W.E.B.

Revolutionary Lives

Series Editors: Sarah Irving, University of Edinburgh;
Professor Paul Le Blanc, La Roche College, Pittsburgh

Revolutionary Lives is a series of short, critical biographies of radical figures from throughout history. The books are sympathetic but not sycophantic, and the intention is to present a balanced and, where necessary, critical evaluation of the individual's place in their political field, putting their actions and achievements in context and exploring issues raised by their lives, such as the use or rejection of violence, nationalism, or gender in political activism. While individuals are the subject of the books, their personal lives are dealt with lightly except insofar as they mesh with political concerns. The focus is on the contribution these revolutionaries made to history, an examination of how far they achieved their aims in improving the lives of the oppressed and exploited, and how they can continue to be an inspiration for many today.

Also available:

Salvador Allende:
Revolutionary Democrat
Victor Figueroa Clark

Hugo Chávez:
Socialist for the Twenty-first Century
Mike Gonzalez

Frantz Fanon:
Philosopher of the Barricades
Peter Hudis

Leila Khaled:
Icon of Palestinian Liberation
Sarah Irvin

Jean Paul Marat:
Tribune of the French Revolution
Clifford D. Conner

Sylvia Pankhurst:
Suffragette, Socialist and Scourge of Empire
Katherine Connelly

Paul Robeson:
A Revolutionary Life
Gerald Horne

Percy Bysshe Shelley:
Poet and Revolutionary
Jacqueline Mulhallen

Ellen Wilkinson:
From Red Suffragist to Government Minister
Paula Bartley

Gerrard Winstanley:
The Digger's Life and Legacy
John Gurney

www.revolutionarylives.co.uk

W.E.B. Du Bois

Revolutionary Across the Color Line

Bill V. Mullen

PlutoPress
www.plutobooks.com

First published 2016 by Pluto Press
345 Archway Road, London N6 5AA

www.plutobooks.com

British Library Cataloguing in Publication Data
A catalogue record for this book is available from the British Library

ISBN	978 0 7453 3506 3	Hardback
ISBN	978 0 7453 3505 6	Paperback
ISBN	978 1 7837 1965 5	PDF eBook
ISBN	978 1 7837 1967 9	Kindle eBook
ISBN	978 1 7837 1966 2	EPUB eBook

This book is printed on paper suitable for recycling and made from fully
managed and sustained forest sources. Logging, pulping and manufacturing
processes are expected to conform to the environmental standards of the
country of origin.

Typeset by Stanford DTP Services, Northampton, England

Simultaneously printed in the European Union and United States of America

Contents

Acknowledgements   vi

Introduction: Revolutionary Lives Matter—Reclaiming
  W.E.B. Du Bois for Our Time   1

PART I: RACIAL UPLIFT AND THE REFORM ERA

1. Childhood, Youth, and Education in an Age of Reform   9
2. Becoming a Scholar and Activist   21
3. Socialism, Activism, and World War I   38

PART II: FROM MOSCOW TO MANCHESTER, 1917–45

4. Du Bois and the Russian Revolution   57
5. The Depression, *Black Reconstruction*, and Du Bois's
    Asia Turn   73
6. Pan-Africanism or Communism?   89

PART III: REVOLUTION AND THE COLD WAR, 1945–63

7. Wrestling with the Cold War, Stalinism, and the Blacklist   107
8. The East is Red: Supporting Revolutions in Asia   123
9. Final Years: Exile, Death, and Legacy   136

Notes   153
Further Reading   168
Index   170

Acknowledgements

The author thanks Paul LeBlanc and Pluto Press for creating the Revolutionary Lives series and for the invitation to contribute to the series.

I am as always in debt to Tithi Bhattacharya for her acumen, political inspiration, insight, and encouragement.

Comrades in the U.S. and around the world have helped my understanding of W.E.B. Du Bois and the revolutionary left in the twentieth century. Their solidarity of ideas and practice informs the interpretation here.

I am grateful to my editor, David Castle, for steerage, guidance and support for this project.

Many scholars and writers have been critical to my analysis of W.E.B. Du Bois as a revolutionary figure. Among them are Keeanga Yamahtta-Taylor, Cedric Robinson, Sharon Smith, Gerald Horne, Robin D.G. Kelley, Brian Jones, Aldon Morris, James Smethurst, the late Fred Ho, David Levering Lewis, Ahmed Shawki, Alex Lubin, Hazel Carby, Alys Weinbaum, Snehal Shingavi, Pranav Jani, Tariq Ali, Deepa Kumar, Benjamin Balthaser, Carol Boyce-Davies, Neil Davidson, Yuichiro Onishi, Estuko Taketani, Alan Wald, Cheryl Higashida, Greg Meyerson, Paul Heideman, Barbara Foley, Ferruccio Gambino.

This book is dedicated to the work of anti-capitalist activists around the world. Their dreams and hopes are the greatest legacy W.E.B. Du Bois could wish for.

Introduction

Revolutionary Lives Matter—
Reclaiming W.E.B. Du Bois for Our Time

Revolution is not a test of capacity; it is always a loss and a lowering of ideals. But if it is a true revolution it repays all losses and results in the uplift of the human race.

—W.E.B. Du Bois, 1962

It is time to cease muting the fact that Dr. Du Bois was a genius and chose to be a Communist. Our irrational obsessive anti-communism had led us into too many quagmires to be retrained as if it were a mode of scientific thinking.

—Dr. Martin Luther King Jr., 1967

In 1951, W.E.B. Du Bois signed his name to "We Charge Genocide," a petition to the United Nations drafted by the radical Civil Rights Congress charging the U.S. with the murder of more than 15 million African-Americans. Subtitled "The Historic Petition to the United Nations for Relief From a Crime of The United States Government Against the Negro People," the petition was inspired by the U.N.'s Convention on the Punishment and Prevention of the Crime of Genocide after the horrors of Nazi Germany's holocaust against Jewish people. The petition's evidence of black genocide included "killings by police . . . killings always on the basis of 'race.'"[1]

"Once the classic method of lynching was the rope," the petition said. "Now it is the policeman's bullet. To many an American the police are the government, certainly its most visible representative. We submit that the evidence suggests that the killing of Negroes has become police policy in the United States and that police policy is the most practical expression of government policy." "We Charge Genocide" also linked state violence against African-Americans to

U.S. imperialism: "White supremacy at home makes for colored massacres abroad. Both reveal contempt for human life in a colored skin. Jellied gasoline in Korea and the lynchers' faggot at home are connected in more ways than that both result in death by fire. The lyncher and the atom bomber are related."[2]

Some 60 years later, in 2011, after the American vigilante George Zimmerman murdered the 17-year-old African-American Travyon Martin, a newly created U.S. activist group named itself "We Charge Genocide" in honor of the 1951 U.N. petition. The Chicago activists documented an epidemic of shootings of African-Americans by police and delivered its evidence to the United Nations Committee Against Torture in Geneva, Switzerland. The group's name, "We Charge Genocide," signified that nothing short of a total transformation of the state's relationship to the people beneath it would suffice. As the Geneva delegation put it, "We see the system as not just broken but fundamentally racist. The problems we see are not things that can be fixed or solved from within that system."[3]

In the world today, too often the public legacy of W.E.B. Du Bois is narrowed to polite advocate of "racial uplift," scholar of African-American history, culture and psychology, or misguided civil rights activist who succumbed in later years to a deformed version of Communism called Stalinism. Rarely remembered is W.E.B. Du Bois the fluid, creative and inspiring revolutionary thinker and activist for global emancipation. In 1919, outraged by the human costs of World War I, but inspired by the Soviet revolution of 1917, Du Bois wrote:

> The one new Idea of the World War—the one which may well stand in future years as the one thing that made the slaughter worthwhile—is an Idea which we are like to fail to know because it is today hidden under the maledictions hurled at Bolshevism. It is not the murder, the anarchy, the hate which for years under Czar and Revolution have drenched this weary land (Russia), but it is the vision of great dreams that only those who work shall vote and rule.[4]

In 1926, upon return from his first visit to the Soviet Union, Du Bois declared, "If what I have seen with my eyes and heard with my ears is

Bolshevism, I am a Bolshevik."⁵ A father of Pan-Africanism, one of the twentieth century's most sustained—and successful—global crusades for freedom, Du Bois was an ardent supporter of every anti-colonial struggle in his lifetime. He declared August 15, 1947, the day of Indian independence, the "greatest historical date of the nineteenth and twentieth centuries."⁶ and hailed China's Communist revolution as one that could help bring about both Asian and African freedom. Along the way, Du Bois pronounced his support for women's social and economic equality, nuclear disarmament, universal public health care, and an end to wars everywhere.

Reasons for the erasure from public view of many of these parts of Du Bois's life and thinking are multiple. He was an early victim of McCarthyism in the U.S., the widespread anti-Communist panic that overtook the United States during the Cold War. In 1951 he was indicted by the U.S. federal government as agent of a foreign state for his work with the Peace Information Center, an anti-nuclear weapons group, and had his passport revoked. During the Cold War, Du Bois's reputation in the capitalist West was stained by his 1961 decision to join the Communist Party of the United States, despite later appeals for tolerance and sympathy of prominent leaders like Martin Luther King, Jr. Du Bois also made errors in political judgment. His support for tyrannical leaders Joseph Stalin and Mao Tse-Tung, and his reticence to publically criticize disasters of Stalinism like the famines it produced and its repression of workers in the name of Communism, have caused many scholars to ignore, shun or caricature Du Bois's lifelong interest in socialism, Marxism, and revolutionary theory and practice.

For these reasons a full accounting of the significance of Du Bois's life for understanding revolution and revolutionary thought in the twentieth century and in our time has eluded us. It is to correct this oversight that this biography exists. *W.E.B. Du Bois: Revolutionary Across the Color Line* examines Du Bois's relationship to key questions of the revolutionary left in the twentieth century: reform versus revolution; socialism and Communism as theories and state practices; the relationship of Communism to anti-colonial movements; the fight against global racism; nationalism and Stalinism; the Cold War and its legacy. To assess these questions, this book situates

Du Bois's life in a new framework, placing him among an international cohort of figures on the global left who advanced the cause of what the Communist International (Comintern) called world revolution—the aspiration to build socialist-inspired revolutions across the globe. These include well-known figures like Jawaharlal Nehru, C.L.R. James, Vladimir Lenin, and George Padmore, and lesser knowns, many of them revolutionary women, like Du Bois's second wife, Shirley Graham Du Bois, who played an influential role in drawing Du Bois to revolutionary politics. One key assertion of this book, downplayed by other Du Bois biographers, is the centrality of radical internationalism to his life and thought. While Du Bois is famous for helping to instigate major U.S. civil rights organizations like the National Association for the Advancement of Colored People (NAACP) and domestic publications like *The Crisis*, his travels to and support for revolution and anti-colonial movements in Russia, Japan, China, and Africa have been marginalized or subordinated to focus on his development as a critic of U.S. race relations. This has served both to domesticate his political perspective and to bleach it of its most radical elements.

W.E.B. Du Bois: Revolutionary Across the Color Line will propose instead that strengths and weaknesses in Du Bois's development of a theory of revolution and revolutionary practice must pay attention to what scholars now call the transnational aspects of his thinking. It argues that Du Bois's sympathies for Stalinism and his idiosyncratic interpretations of Comintern Marxism, for example, were related to efforts to develop revolutionary paradigms to apply to the lives of African-Americans. For example, Du Bois's majestic study of the Civil War and the end of slavery, *Black Reconstruction*, applied Du Bois's enthusiasm for national liberation struggles and national self-determination onto African-American efforts at self-emancipation during and after formal emancipation. The book also overturned nearly 100 years of racist writing and scholarship on slavery and the Civil War, and offered one of the first interpretations of the role of American capitalism and slavery in the formation of U.S. imperialism and Western colonialism. It remains to this day a classic in the history of Marxist scholarship. Or to take another example, Du Bois's attempts in the 1930s to develop a theory and practice of black economic cooperatives in the U.S. were inspired by examples from Russia, Israel, and Japan, among other places.

This book will thus examine both Du Bois's creative additions to the theory and practice of revolution in the twentieth century and to Marxist theory. It recognizes Du Bois's analysis of twentieth-century revolutions as both precursors and cautionary tales for our own times. In addition to his groundbreaking work against state violence cited above, Du Bois's writing remain relevant to our assessment of ongoing struggles in the former colonial world (like Egypt and India), and to analysis of the horrors of contemporary capitalism and neoliberalism Du Bois's own work magnificently foretold. This book will also more thoroughly explore the later years of Du Bois's official Communist turn both to illuminate the effects of the Cold War on his career and to make explicit Du Bois's wrongheaded, if ambivalent, dedication to Stalinized revolutions in Russia and China especially.

In addition, the book will explore contradictions in Du Bois's political thought that were part of his evolution from reformist and bourgeois democrat to radical Socialist. Du Bois began his life and career under the influence of Pan-Africanists, social democrats and race liberals who tried first to use parliamentary and democratic means to achieve progress on matters of racism and economic reform. He was early on very skeptical of the revolutionary potential of the working class. Thus missing from Du Bois's early life and thought was a dedication to a view of the working class as an agent of its own emancipation. His early elitism also caused him to look for top-down solutions to political problems. This led Du Bois into political misjudgments, like his support for Woodrow Wilson in the 1912 U.S. presidential election, and later to support for Joseph Stalin.

Finally, the book will make central the importance of political revolution, and world revolution, in Du Bois's thought, aspects made ever more critical to our understanding in the wake of triumphant— and failed—recent popular revolutions in Tunisia and Egypt, of recent waves of worker uprisings in Spain and Greece, and ongoing liberation movements in Syria and Palestine. Especially towards the end of his life, the period least examined by scholars and biographers, Du Bois developed an emancipatory vision of revolution descended from Marx but cast in a quasi-utopian—or messianic—framework reminiscent of the writings of the German Marxist Walter Benjamin.[7] Like Benjamin, Du Bois struggled with the catastrophes of world wars, anti-semitic purges, imperialism and genocide as challenges to Western narratives of historical progress. It was in search of a resolution to what he called in *Black Reconstruction* "counter-revolutions" of history that Du Bois himself landed on the idea of world revolution itself as a plan to support. In the end, Du Bois chose socialism, declaring, "I seek a world where the ideals of communism will triumph—to each according to his need, from each according to his ability."[8] In his own biography of Du Bois, David Levering Lewis suggests that Du Bois's revolutionary aspirations for the twentieth century bear special promise, instruction and weight for our own in the twenty-first. He writes, "while the historically specific state socialist project through which Du Bois hoped his reconstruction of democracy would happen founders on the ruins of the Soviet Union and on Russia's and China's free markets and imperialist adventures in the present, the project of transforming the state to better promote economic and racial justice remains a necessity."[9]

Lewis poses what might be called central contradictions and aspirations guiding this book. Du Bois's devotion to the idea of world revolution, anti-colonialism and racial and economic democracy was an ambition that came with struggles, and at times mistakes, in assessing how that revolution should best occur. His desire to see the wretched of the earth rise through self-emancipation at times blinded him to moments of political catastrophe like the Cultural Revolution and the errors and horrors of Stalinism. These characteristics put him in common with among the most important revolutionaries of the past century, the century of the global color line. Yet for the revolutionary left, Du Bois is most important because of his unwavering commitment to the elimination of social inequality, the end to racism, and the abolition of the destructiveness of imperialist wars. In this regard the legacy and inspiration of W.E.B. Du Bois, fully understood, may help us out of our current conjuncture of post-colonial inequality, hyper-capitalist exploitation, environmental destruction, global-scale xenophobia and racism, misogyny and "endless war." This work will seek to take up these questions through offering a new interpretation of the revolutionary life of W.E.B. Du Bois.

PART I

RACIAL UPLIFT AND THE REFORM ERA

1

Childhood, Youth, and Education in an Age of Reform

"I was born by a golden river and in the shadow of two great hills, five years after the Emancipation Proclamation, which began the freeing of American Negro slaves."[1] So begins Chapter VI, "My Birth and Family," of W.E.B. Du Bois's posthumously published *Autobiography*. Typically, Du Bois renders his life as a symbol of both African-American history and the wider struggle for black freedom. This was a conceit well earned from the beginning of Du Bois's days—February 21, 1868—to their end, August 28, 1963.

Du Bois descended on his maternal side from the "black Burghardts," Africans descended from Tom Burghardt, born in West Africa around 1730, and stolen by Dutch slave traders for transport to America. Tom grew up in the service of the white Burghardt family in the Hudson Valley area of New York state in the northeastern United States. Enlisted service in the American revolutionary army freed Tom Burghardt from slavery before his death around 1787 (It was not until 1817 that New York, a northern state, formally emancipated its slaves). The Burghardts who followed Tom worked as farmers, barbers, waiters, cooks, housemaids, and laborers. Du Bois's mother, Mary Silvina, was born in 1831. "She gave one the impression of infinite patience, but a curious detachment was concealed in her softness" Du Bois recalled of her in *Darkwater*.[2] Yet over time she became, recalls Du Bois, a "silent, repressed woman, working at household duties at home, helping now and then in the neighbors' homes."[3]

When Mary was 35, Alfred Du Bois came to her small town of Great Barrington, Massachusetts. First settled by American colonists, Great Barrington was known for being a leisure retreat for the wealthy. Alfred's grandfather was Dr. James Du Bois, a white American physician who while in the Bahamas either took as his slave a concubine or married a free Negro woman. Alexander Du Bois, Alfred's father, lived in Haiti from 1821 to 1830 before settling in New Haven, Connecticut. In 1867, when Alfred arrived in Great Barrington, he was disliked by the black Burghardts. "He had apparently no property and no job" wrote Du Bois, "and they had never heard of the Du Bois family in New York." Nevertheless Mary and Alfred took up a "runaway marriage"[4] and within a year, William Edward Burghardt Du Bois was born.

By the time Mary and Alfred married, the area around Great Barrington was transitioning from an agricultural to an industrial and domestic labor economy. Du Bois was born in a home owned by an ex-slave who had like many African-Americans come north after emancipation as part of that transition. Du Bois's racially mixed ancestry made him from birth a curiosity in a country obsessed since the time of slavery with racial identity. For example, slaves were defined as African-Americans with "one drop" of black blood. Thus, "I was of great interest to the whole town" Du Bois wrote. "The whites waited to see 'when my hair was going to curl.'"[5] Despite the fact that Great Barrington's population was less than 5 percent black (census records indicate there were probably about 20 black families in Great Barrington) it was the socio-economic, not racial, conditions of his early upbringing that first stood out to the young Du Bois. "I had, as a child, almost no experience of segregation or color discrimination."[6] Yet Du Bois noted that he and his mother lived "near the edge of poverty"[7] a condition which Du Bois wrote put him in line with many Great Barrington villagers who were poor or lower middle class. Many of these poor were Irish and Eastern European laborers who, like African-Americans, were among the poorest of the Great Barrington community. Du Bois in fact admitted to a certain snobbery in his own attitudes towards some poor immigrants. "I did not then associate poverty or ignorance with color, but rather with lack of opportunity; or more often with lack of thrift."[8] This early moralistic philosophy, characteristic of what Max Weber called the "Protestant ethic," was one which would be challenged by events to come.

Without question the greatest influence on Du Bois's development in his early years was his mother Mary. Du Bois's father Alfred, whose trade was barbering, did not stay with the family long. He was in Du Bois's memory "a dreamer—romantic, indolent, kind, unreliable"[9] and given to writing poetry. Du Bois later speculated that color prejudice, or what might be called "colorism" by the Burghardts may have contributed to his departure—they were lighter-skinned than he. Du Bois also had a brother, Idelbert, about whom he said and wrote very little. Du Bois's Uncle Othello, who he remembered as "probably a bit lazy and given to wassail"[10] died when Du Bois was very young, worsening the family's financial prospects. The lives of these black men were also likely shaped by discrimination; during this period of industrialization in New England black workers were routinely kept out of factory jobs, and black women were generally relegated to work as domestic servants. Yet because she recognized both his academic ability and his discipline, Mary Silvina doted on her son and urged him on in school, all the while working various jobs, including domestic, to support him. When Du Bois was about ten, Mary decided to move them from their shabby home surrounded by bars and gambling clubs to a small home nearer the river, where they lived with Mary's brother William. Du Bois did odd jobs like mowing lawns to contribute to the family income in keeping with his orientation to Puritan thrift and self-sufficiency. This was necessary as Mary's income was barely sufficient to pay the rent and her health was often poor. At one point she suffered a stroke from which she never fully recovered. For a time, Du Bois and Mary lived in his maternal grandfather's home with its "stone fireplace, big kitchen, and delightful woodshed."[11] In 1884, when he was just 16, Mary died, and Du Bois went to live with an aunt.

By all accounts of his childhood, including his own, Du Bois worked and studied more than he socialized; most of his childhood memories involved achievement of small goals of reading or writing, though he did purport to be "a center and sometimes the leader of the town gang of boys."[12] Du Bois took part in ordinary mischief, once nearly sent to reform school for being part of a group of boys who took some grapes from the young of a wealthy white man until his school principal, Frank Hosmer, intervened on his behalf. Hosmer gained

Du Bois's affections for advocating for his education and training to become a possible leader of other African-Americans. He helped to place Du Bois in a college preparatory program. Throughout this childhood Du Bois showed little interest in money or career. "Wealth had no particular lure," he wrote.[13]

A memorable episode in the development of race consciousness in Du Bois's childhood is recounted in *The Souls of Black Folk* when at the age of ten he is jolted by the refusal of a white girl at school into a foreshadowing of his understanding of his difference and distance from the majority world around him:

> I remember well when the shadow swept across me. I was a little thing, away up in the hills of New England, where the dark Housatonic winds between Hoosac and Taghkanic to the sea. In a wee wooden school house, something put it into the boys' and girls' heads to buy gorgeous visiting cards—ten cents a package— and exchange. The exchange was merry, till one girl, a taller newcomer, refused my card—refused it peremptorily with a glance. Then it dawned upon me with a certain suddenness that I was different from the others; or like, mayhap, in heart and life, and longing, but shut out from their world by a vast veil.[14]

This episode was a reminder that Du Bois was often the only African-American in his school classes, and that generic racial prejudice were part of the fabric of Great Barrington town life. Du Bois described his feeling of exclusion for the first time in *The Souls of Black Folk* as a contempt for those who would demean him. He determined to beat his white counterparts at anything he could, while protecting himself from the demoralization of "silent hatred" some of his black contemporaries came to learn. Looking back on this adolescence, Du Bois was made to feel white supremacy at the most personal level—it was local prejudice rather than hardened racism as he perceived it—and it is clear that he began to draw up inside a reserve to allow him to thrive. As he put it:

> Very gradually,—I cannot now distinguish the steps, though here and there I remember a jump or a jot—but very gradually

I found myself assuming quite placidly that I was different from other children. At first I think I connected the difference with a manifest ability to get my lessons rather better than most and to recite with a certain happy, almost taunting, blindness, which brought frowns here and there. Then, slowly, I realized that some folks, a few even, even several, actually considered my brown skin a misfortune; once or twice I became painfully aware that some human beings even thought it a crime. I was not for a moment daunted,—although, of course, there were some days of secret tears—rather I was spurred to tireless effort. If they beat me at anything, I was grimly determined to make them sweat for it![15]

By the age of 15, two distinctive patterns emerged in Du Bois's life that reflect his spirited response to racism. First was his exceptional academic performance. "Gradually I became conscious that in most of the school work my natural gifts and regular attendance made me rank among the best, so that my promotions were regular and expected."[16] Du Bois was in fact something of an academic prodigy, even recognized by his white teachers for his exceptional abilities. The second was an urge to write and publish. In April 1883, Du Bois debuted as Great Barrington correspondent to the New York *Globe*, an African-American weekly newspaper edited by Timothy Thomas Fortune. Fortune was a radical reformer who founded the militant civil rights organization the National Afro-American League. Du Bois's first publication in the *Globe* was a short news item urging African-American men of Great Barrington to join a new "Law and Order society" to enforce laws against liquor selling.[17] The article is the first public glimpse of Du Bois's youthful brand of Victorian reformism. In all, Du Bois would make 27 contributions to Fortune's paper between 1883 and 1885. In one of these we get a further glimpse into Du Bois's rising social and intellectual profile in the town: a report that he will take part in a local debate on the question, "Which is of the more use to a country, the Warrior, the Statesman, or the Poet?"—a reference to Percy Shelley's famous formulation.[18]

Another figure who influenced Du Bois's budding career as an intellectual was a local historian, Charles Taylor, who had published a history of Great Barrington. Du Bois's affinity for Taylor was clear evidence of his desperate desire to find intellectual and scholarly inspiration in a small Great Barrington community of about 4,000 people. In *The Souls of Black Folk*, he would turn this autobiographical quest for knowledge into a parable of the wider yearning of the black race for education, formal schooling and "book learning" after emancipation.

Du Bois graduated high school in 1884 the only African-American student in his class. The subject of his commencement oration was the life of anti-slavery agitator Wendell Phillips, one of Du Bois's early heroes. It is important to note that 1884, the year of his commencement, was only 19 years after the end of the Civil War, and only seven years since the end of Reconstruction, the federal government plan to rebuild the South after the war to be discussed in detail later. Du Bois's childhood and adolescence, in other words, was lived in the shadow of slavery, and in a period of enormous national anxiety for both blacks and whites about the future of race relations. Du Bois's commitment to the study of the anti-slavery movement and figures like Phillips was symbolic of this moment of transformation and his own budding political consciousness. At the same time, Du Bois's early years were heavily shaped by the dominant mores of New England society. He thought of himself, in non-pejorative terms, as a native son of the United States, something of an aspiring intellectual rooted not necessarily in a black tradition of social resistance, to which he had not yet been exposed, but of general cultural learning characteristic of nineteenth-century literature society. He was in other words, for a black man of his time, extraordinary in his gifts, talents and aspirations, but in other regards for an American of the lower-middle classes, somewhat typical.

Encouraged by his mother and his own ambitions, Du Bois aspired to go to Harvard, hoping to reach the pinnacle of academic success, but his high school was below the University's entrance requirements. In defiance of his family's "Northern free Negro prejudice" against attending school in the "former land of slavery," Du Bois enrolled instead at Fisk University in Nashville, Tennessee. The decision was Du Bois's first small rebellion against his New England upbringing, and showed his desire to enter the national post-Civil War stream of African-American racial uplift—the idea that through hard work, civic participation, and race leadership the lives of African-Americans could be improved.

Fisk had been established just three months after the signing of the Emancipation Proclamation to provide higher education to newly-freed slaves. The establishment of what came to be known as "Historically Black Colleges and Universities" was itself part of the federal government Reconstruction effort. In explaining his decision to attend, Du Bois wrote, "Black folk were bound in time to play a large role in the South. They needed trained leadership. I was sent to help furnish it."[19] Du Bois also found his personality and emotional life expanded and liberated by stepping for the first time into a bustling all-black world:

Consider, for a moment, how miraculous it all was to a boy of seventeen, just escaped from a narrow valley: I will and lo! my people came dancing about me,—riotous in color, gay in laughter, full of sympathy, need, and pleading; darkly delicious girls— "colored" girls—sat beside me and actually talked to me while I gazed in tongue-tied silence or babbled in boastful dreams. Boys with my own experience and out of my own world, who knew and understood, wrought out with me great remedies. I studied eagerly under teachers who bent in subtle sympathy, feeling themselves some shadow of the Veil and lifting it gently that we darker souls might peer through to other worlds.[20]

At the same time, Du Bois's arrival for the first time in the South also triggered new ideas in his young mind about race and national identity:

I came to a region where the world was split into white and black halves, and where the darker half was held back by race prejudice and legal bonds, as well as by deep ignorance and dire poverty. But facing this was not a lost group, but at Fisk, a microcosm of a world and civilization in potentiality. Into this world I leapt with enthusiasm. A new loyalty and allegiance replaced my Americanism: hence-forward I was a Negro.[21]

Du Bois's first encounter with Jim Crow thus produced a sense of what he calls in his famous 1903 book *The Souls of Black Folk* "double consciousness," a feeling that to be "an American, a negro" at the same time was to feel a sense of "twoness." His trip to the deeply segregated South also introduced a sharper feeling of alienation from the United States Eric Porter has called Du Bois's "disidentificatory Americanism."[22] Du Bois initially embraced a strong group or "race" consciousness as a buffer against these effects, while perceiving that consciousness as a pathway into what he calls here "a world and civilization in potentiality."

These ideas help us locate Du Bois within larger currents of his time. At his commencement from Fisk in June 1888, Du Bois chose German Chancellor Otto Von Bismarck as the subject of his oration. "The choice in itself," Du Bois later wrote, "showed the abyss between my education and the truth in the world. Bismarck was my hero. He had made a nation out of a mass of bickering peoples."[23] "This foreshadowed in my mind the kind of thing that American Negroes must do, marching forth with strength and determination under trained leadership."[24] Initially missing from Du Bois's embrace of these ideas was any analysis of the costs of nation-building in the form of wars, empire-building, and slavery. Wrote Du Bois, "I was blithely European and imperialist in outlook . . . I do not remember ever hearing Karl Marx mentioned nor socialism discussed."[25]

The conflict generated by racial alienation, on the one hand, and a longing for group solidarity on the other, followed Du Bois to Harvard—"the college of my youngest, wildest visions!"[26]—where he successfully transferred to complete his B.A. degree after his Fisk education. So did Du Bois's sense of his own life as an upwardly mobile reformer capable of leading African-Americans. As he put it on his arrival, "I went to Harvard as a Negro, not simply by birth, but recognizing myself as a member of a segregated caste whose situation I accepted but was determined to work from within that caste to find my way out."[27] In the classroom, the philosopher William James, brother of the novelist Henry James, piqued his interest in philosophical pragmatism, and he learned what he later called "reactionary economics of the Ricardo school." English political economist David Ricardo had become famous for writing how capitalism and free trade functioned to improve the human condition while paying little attention to the inequalities it produced. Meanwhile, wrote Du Bois, "Karl Marx was mentioned but only incidentally and as one whose doubtful theories had long since been refuted. Socialism as dream of philanthropy or as will-o-wisp of hotheads was dismissed as unimportant."[28]

The tension between a nineteenth-century liberal education and his increasing group attachment with an oppressed race—Du Bois called it "protective self-coloration"—flared dramatically in his 1890 Harvard commencement address on Jefferson Davis, President of the Confederacy (the secessionist southern government) during the Civil War. Titled "Jefferson Davis as Representative of Civilization," the essay asserts Du Bois's first dialectical interpretation of history.[29] Whereas Du Bois's adulation for Bismarck and nation-building had been literally one-sided in its praise, here Du Bois perceives in the "Teutonic Hero" of Davis a "type of civilization" built upon the ruins of imperialism, slavery and racism: "It made a naturally brave and generous man—Jefferson Davis—now advancing civilization by murdering Indians, now hero of national disgrace called by courtesy, the Mexican War; and finally, as the crowning absurdity, the peculiar champion of a people fighting to be free in order that another people should not be free."[30]

Du Bois here also advances a criticism of the "civilizationist" discourse that had led him to Bismarck in the first place. "The Teutonic met civilization and crushed it—the Negro met civilization and was crushed by it."[29] And then:

> No matter how great and striking the Teutonic type of impetuous manhood may be, it must receive the cool purposeful "Ich Dien" of the African for its round and full development. In the rise of Negro people and development of this idea, you whose Nation was founded on the loftiest ideals, and who many times forgot those ideals with a strange forgetfulness, have more than a sentimental interest, more than a sentimental duty. You owe a debt to humanity for this Ethiopia of the Outstretched Arm, who has made her beauty, patience, and her grandeur, law.[30]

Du Bois's reference to the ancient African state of Ethiopia as the fountainhead of black civilization foreshadowed two new directions in his thought. The first was the ambition to develop a system of measurement for African contribution to Western world history. That would lead him to become co-founder of the Pan-African Movement in 1900, and to his first book on Africa, *The Negro*, published in 1915. The second was deeper analysis of the transatlantic slave trade. In 1890, he would choose as the topic for his doctoral thesis the suppression of the African slave trade to America. He was appointed a Henry Bromfield Rogers fellow, which sustained his studies on this work at Harvard from 1890 to 1892. The dissertation, completed in 1895, was the first scholarly study of slavery by a black scholar in the U.S. Du Bois documented U.S. participation in the slave trade, the number of Africans enslaved, and slave resistance in a chapter on Toussaint L'Ouverture and the Haitian Revolution of 1798–1804, the first successful black revolution in the modern world. The Haitian Revolution would become a recurring inspiration for Du Bois's conception of black revolution and revolutionary historiography as it would for his contemporaries like C.L.R. James. Yet Du Bois later lamented that the dissertation was written with no knowledge of Marxism which made him "miss the clear conclusion that slavery was more a matter of income than morals."[31]

Despite undertaking his undergraduate and graduate studies in an era which "to my mind and the minds of most of my teachers" was "a day of Progress with a capital P," Du Bois saw beneath the surface of his studies. "We studied history and politics almost exclusively from the point of view of ancient German freedom, English and New England democracy, and the development of the white United States."[32] The 1884 Berlin Conference at which European countries had partitioned Africa while "colonies were being seized and countries integrated into European civilization in Asia, Africa, South America, and the islands" was one of the events which made him curious to study abroad.

In 1892, he received a Slater Fund fellowship to attend the University of Berlin. Du Bois fought hard to earn a Slater Fund fellowship—"I went at them hammer and tongs!"[33]—becoming the first African-American to achieve one. Suddenly "on the outside of the American world, looking in," his racial and political perspective was shattered. "The unity beneath all life clutched me. I was not less fanatically a Negro, but 'Negro' meant a greater, broader sense of humanity and world fellowship."[34] Intellectual and political triggers for this new point of view were provided by lectures and seminars with Gustav Schmoller. He was introduced to quantitative methods of research and began his training as a sociologist. Du Bois had also come to Germany in part to study agrarian relationships to modern capitalism because of the role of African-Americans in southern agriculture, slavery, and sharecropping. As Aldon Morris notes, "These issues were germane to Du Bois because he had decided that his life's mission was to help liberate African-Americans from racial oppression."[35] Du Bois would write his thesis in Berlin on the topic "The Large and Small-scale System of Agriculture in the Southern United States, 1840–1890." One of his mentors wrote about his thesis "The work proves that the author possesses talent and diligence, and that he has made good use of the time spent in Germany."[36] Much scholarship on Du Bois insists that he came under the influence of the German sociologist Max Weber, enrolled as a student at the same time as Du Bois in Berlin, but the two were more peers rather than student–teacher. For bureaucratic reasons, Du Bois was not able to take a Ph.D. from the University, a disappointment that may later have informed the plot of his novel *Dark Princess*, which begins with his protagonist unable to complete his medical studies.

Du Bois's arrival in Germany also came on the heels of German Kaiser Wilhelm II's decision to allow socialists to publically organize, ending their illegality under Bismarck. Du Bois frequently attended meetings of the new socialist Social Democratic Party (SDP) in the working-class district of Pankow.[37] But the dominance in the SDP of the revisionist, reformist and anarchist ideas of Ferdinand Lassalle, Eduard Bernstein, and Mikhail Bakunin slowed Du Bois's first efforts to understand Marxism's central ideas of surplus value and surplus labor, and of workers taking over the means of production and seizing state power. As he put it, "I was overwhelmed with rebuttals of Marxism before I understood the original doctrine."[38] Du Bois later lamented that his academic work prevented him from fulling engaging with workers in Germany and learning more of their plight.

He also said that fine distinctions between the thought of Marx and SDP leaders like Karl Kautsky were "too complicated for a student like myself to understand."[39] Still, exposure to the internationalist character of both Marxism and the Second International began to alter Du Bois's thinking. "I began to see the race problem in America, the problems of the peoples of Africa and Asia, and the political development of Europe as one."[40]

Du Bois's evolution from small-town prodigy to international scholar in the course of 25 years is remarkable. His self-discipline and motivation coupled with his ability to dream beyond the boundaries of racism and racial provincialism would become keynotes of the rest of his life. His tenacious commitment to self-education, on one hand, and commitment to the study of African-American history foreshadow a century of personal—and group—achievement in intellectual and political life. Unconsciously but deliberately, Du Bois was making himself a "race man" to be emulated by other African-Americans to follow. Du Bois's early travels from New England to the South to Europe also foreshadow his life as a globetrotting intellectual and political activist who would eventually visit the Caribbean, Africa, and China. This worldly knowledge helped to develop Du Bois's dedication to anti-colonialism and world revolution. By 1915, Du Bois would explain the origins of World War I as inter-imperialist rivalry and the "scramble for Africa" launched by the European powers in 1884. Within a few years, Du Bois would throw his endorsement to Japan as a rising power in Asia to combat white supremacy. Still, in 1894, when Du Bois returned from Berlin to America, he was mainly committed to capitalizing on his formal education by establishing work and a career, and deciding how to use his training to generate reforms to benefit the majority of African-Americans still living under Jim Crow—formal, legal segregation—in the American South. This was the main challenge he wrote, of being "dropped back suddenly into 'nigger'-hating America!"[41]

2

Becoming a Scholar and Activist

Du Bois returned to the U.S. from Germany in 1894 at the age of 26. As he wrote in his *Autobiography*, "It was a disturbed world in which I landed."[1] The 1890s were a peak time for black lynchings in the U.S., brought on by the demise of Reconstruction—the U.S. federal government program to assist freed slaves in the post-Civil War South—and the emergence of white supremacist groups like the Ku Klux Klan. In 1895, "Jim Crow" or formal segregation became legal southern doctrine as a result of the Supreme Court "Plessy Versus Ferguson" ruling that "separate but equal" conditions for blacks and whites were constitutional. The name Jim Crow came from a nineteenth-century minstrel dancer who would "Dance Jim Crow."

Despite holding a Harvard doctoral degree, Du Bois's job prospects were limited by racism. He wrote to no white institution for teaching positions—"I knew there were no openings."[2] After making application to Howard, Hampton, Tuskegee, and other historically black colleges created after the Civil War to educate freed slaves, he received a teaching offer from the Classics Department at Wilberforce University in Ohio. Wilberforce was a "small colored denominational college"[3] operated by the national African Methodist Church, one of the largest in the United States. Du Bois was hired to teach Latin, Greek, German, and English. He arrived at Wilberforce full of idealism and wanting to "help build a great university," but soon realized the school's poor finances and church-driven mission put limits on academic achievement for himself and his students.

In 1896, while still at Wilberforce, Du Bois married Nina Gomer, who had been one of his students. She was one of three children born to a hotel chef and his wife. Much of Gomer's life was confined to domestic responsibility for Du Bois and their two children: Burghardt, who died tragically at the age of two in 1899, and a daughter,

Scurlock Studio (Washington, D.C.). Nina (Gomer) Du Bois, c. 1940. W.E.B. Du Bois Papers (MS 312). Special Collections and University Archives, University of Massachusetts Amherst Libraries

Yolande, born in 1900. While she was not a public activist, Gomer's personal writings do indicate a strong anger against racism faced in her private life. Typically, though, Du Bois downplayed the role of Nina (and other women) in his life development. Nina is described in his *Autobiography* as a "slip of a girl, beautifully dark-eyed" and the marriage takes up less than a paragraph. The responsibility of supporting himself and Nina, however, was partial motivation for Du Bois accepting in the fall of 1896 an offer as "assistant instructor" at the University of Pennsylvania. This appointment also reflected the racism of the period. Du Bois was hired by the Department of Sociology to research what white city fathers called "The corrupt, semi-criminal vote of the Negro Seventh Ward," the heavily African-American district of Philadelphia, which they blamed for political corruption in the city.[4] Du Bois accepted the task because he had a strong desire to conduct sociological study of African-Americans and to fight back against racist academic studies of their lives. As Du Bois put it, "The world was thinking wrong about race, because it did not know. The ultimate evil was stupidity. The cure for it was knowledge based on scientific investigation."[5] Or as Aldon Morris has put it, "Du Bois was aware that white sociologists possessed little knowledge of black institutions and cultural processes. They tended to view black communities as distorted and inferior copies of white communities."[6]

In 1897, Du Bois along with the African-American scholar and missionary Alexander Crummell, helped to co-found the American Negro Academy. Du Bois had first met Crummell when the latter served as commencement speaker at Wilberforce. The Episcopal priest and scholar had spent nearly 20 years doing mission work in Liberia where he supported both the Christianization of the native population and the repatriation of African-Americans to the colony founded by former slaves. Crummell, along with Henry Highland Garnet and Martin Robinson Delany, were all known to Du Bois as proponents of early versions of Pan-Africanism and black nationalism. In *The Souls of Black Folk*, Du Bois wrote admiringly of Crummell as an exemplar of the black scholar he himself hoped to become.

The American Negro Academy was itself largely Crummell's idea. Du Bois was among the original cohort of planners which included the distinguished African-American poet Paul Laurence Dunbar and the Howard University philosopher Kelly Miller. The all-male body of African-American scholars sought to promote research and learning on the conditions of African-American life. The Academy was also meant to be a space for criticism of the ideas of Booker T. Washington. Washington had already opened his Tuskegee Institute dedicated to the idea of vocational training as a means of racial uplift for African-Americans. Crummell, in contrast, sought to promote the Academy as a place for African-American participation in high culture, science, philosophy and letters. Crummell's inaugural address to the Academy was entitled "Civilization: The Primal Need of the Race." In 1908, when Crummell died, Du Bois was voted President of the Academy.

From 1897–1924, the Academy published a number of scholarly studies of slavery, the conditions of black life in the United States, and the meaning of race in the U.S. The Academy's significance was largely confined to the development of black academic life while heralding a new era of African-American scholarship of which Du Bois was a key part.

Important to this study, the Academy was also directly formative of what Du Bois later termed his own "talented tenth" concept of training a small layer of black leadership from African-American society to lead and guide the rest. As with the Academy, Du Bois's idea was meant to differentiate a social program for black achievement that would refuse the limits of Washington's vocational training program and its concomitant subordination of questions of civil and social rights. Among the allies in this early conception for Du Bois were figures like the abolitionist publisher Ida B. Wells-Barnet and William Trotter, who saw black education and higher education in particular as a key to the social transformation of black life. Du Bois articulated the "Talented Tenth" idea in two places first: in the essay "Of Mr. Booker T. Washington and Others" in *The Souls of Black Folk* and in the essay "Of the Training of Black Men." Du Bois flatly dismissed the idea that mere manual training and employment would be sufficient for black freedom. As he put it in the essay "The Talented Tenth", published the same year as *The Souls of Black Folk*, "The Negro race, like all races, is going to be saved by its exceptional men . . . Was there ever a nation on God's fair earth civilized from the bottom upward? Never; it is, ever was, and ever will be from the top downward that culture filters."[7]

Du Bois's formulation of the "Talented Tenth" was also central to the wider program at the turn of the century of what became known as "racial uplift" doctrine. That idea argued that African-Americans of exceptional talent and social positioning would best be suited to lead the race forward. For example, Du Bois argued that Washington's failure to assert the need for higher education for African-Americans was doomed to limit black potential. While Booker T. Washington was a foil for the argument, the idea drew in a wide range of African-American reformers, intellectuals and activists. These would include leaders of the Pan-African movement like British barrister Henry

Sylvester Williams, poet Paul Laurence Dunbar, scholar John Hope, a black educator and first president of Morehouse College; novelist Charles Chesnutt, author of the well-regarded 1899 book *The Conjure Woman*. Du Bois did not initially extend credit for their work to female contemporaries like anti-lynching activist and publisher Ida B. Wells-Barnett, integrationist Mary Terrell, and author Jessie Redmon Fauset, who would later join Du Bois as an editor on *The Crisis*, but by 1920 they too would constitute a layer of "Talented Tenth" black leadership. Of this group, Wells-Barnett was perhaps closest to Du Bois in her explicit rejection of Washington's "bootstrap" theory of self-help. She would subsequently become one of two women to sign on their initial support for the foundation of the National Association for the Advancement of Colored People (NAACP). Significant to note is that most of these leaders hailed from backgrounds of relative prosperity and had achieved professional standing, thus making their success and uplift theory a foreshadowing of what would later be called black "respectability" politics, emphasizing the need for achievement, upward mobility and, to some degree, assimilation into mainstream dominant society.

Crummell's insistence on the concept of black contribution to "civilization" development was also, importantly, a key influence on Du Bois's thinking about race. For Crummell, black culture and intellectual history was an autonomous national tradition unto itself. Crummell's idea should be understood as a prototype of what was to become black nationalist thinking in the twentieth century. Crummell's thought merged for Du Bois with his own developing simultaneous consideration on the meaning of race as it was being elaborated in nineteenth-century science. Thus, significantly, it was to the American Negro Academy in 1897 that Du Bois presented his early essay "The Conservation of Races." The essay is the most serious attempt by the young Du Bois to adopt to his own thinking on race, civilization and eighteenth- and nineteenth-century classificatory science by scholars like Thomas Henry Huxley and Friedrich Raetzel:

> . . . the history of the world is the history, not of individuals, but of groups, not of nations, but of races, and he who ignores or seeks to override the race idea in human history ignores and overrides

the central thought of all history. What, then, is a race? It is a vast family of human beings, generally of common blood and language, always of common history, traditions and impulses, who are both voluntarily and involuntarily striving together for the accomplishment of certain more or less vividly conceived ideals of life.[8]

Affirming that "Negroes of Africa and America" were a racial group enabled Du Bois to identify both the "common history, traditions and impulses" and "ideals of life" of a people understood to have a unique historical mission and purpose: "For the development of Negro genius, of Negro literature and art, of Negro spirit, only Negroes bound and welded together, Negroes inspired by one vast ideal, can work out in its fullness the great message we have for humanity."

More important, Du Bois's demand for the "conservation" of the race was central to a social strategy for group advancement:

. . . we are Negroes, members of a vast historic race that from the very dawn of creation has slept, but half awakening in the dark forests of the African fatherland . . . As such, it is our duty to conserve our physical powers, our intellectual endowments, our spiritual ideas; as a race we must strive by race organization, by race solidarity, by race unity to the realization of that broader humanity which freely recognizes differences in men, but sternly deprecates inequalities in their opportunities of development.[9]

For Du Bois, building "race organization" meant developing groups like the American Negro Academy, and "race solidarity" required civil rights organizations. This explains his decision within just a few years to help organize the NAACP and the Niagara Movement. The word "strive" by 1897 was already synonymous in public discourse with "racial uplift" philosophy. "Uplifting the race," as scholar Kevin Gaines has noted, was the largely bourgeois ideology of group self-improvement through gradual reform of social and economic conditions under guidance of outstanding individual "race leaders" themselves drawn from black elites.[10] The word "strive" captured perfectly that straining for mobility. At the same time, Du Bois's confidence in "race organization" indicated a need to address the prevailing racial problem in America at this time: racial segregation. It must be remembered that the American Negro Academy and "The Conservation of Races" were produced exactly two years after the Plessy versus Ferguson decision which gave legal sanction to "Jim Crow" segregation in the South. How northern, urban elites could respond in theory practice to the new sufferings of their southern black brothers and sisters was also an implied challenge for "race leaders" like Du Bois.

These ideas and problems influenced Du Bois's sociology of the "Negro" in Philadelphia's Seventh Ward. He argued that the historical experience of African-Americans was unique and should be assessed on its own terms, something no other sociologist had argued before. Du Bois was also influenced by the development in cities like Chicago of new "Settlement Houses" like Hull House that conducted sociological study while providing social assistance to impoverished groups of citizens and migrants. Influenced by the Settlement mission and its literature, Du Bois's book was intended to be a guide to the uplift and reform of black lives in Philadelphia.

The Philadelphia Negro argues that while there were other "unassimilated groups" in the city like Jews and Italians, "in the case of the Negroes the segregation is more conspicuous, more patent to the eye, and so intertwined with a long historic evolution, with peculiarly pressing social problems of poverty, ignorance, crime and labor, that the Negro problem far surpassed in scientific interest and social gravity most of the other race or class questions."[11] His book then offers a "plan of presentment" in four parts: history of the African-American population in the city; "present condition considered as individuals;" "condition as an organized social group;" "physical and social environment." Aligning himself with Progressive Era ideology, Du Bois presented his findings as a case study for "practical reform"[12] of African-American living conditions. Yet the text of *The Philadelphia Negro* moves back and forth between Du Bois's efforts to destroy social stereotypes of the "Negro group as a symptom, not a cause; as a striving, palpitating group, and not an inert, sick body of crime"[13] and a residual Victorian moralism and "uplift" elitism that tends to reinforce those same stereotypes.

For example, in trying to dispel negative stereotypes of black people as responsible for their own poverty, Du Bois presented vivid historical explanations of African-American migration to the city as untrained and poorly educated fugitive slave and freemen after Emancipation; described spatial segregation of the African-American population by city elites into "slums"—one of the first usages of that term in scholarship; pointed to the relegation of black labor to low-paid, unskilled work; cited low rates of home ownership and unequal black access to health care, sanitation and healthy living. "Race prejudice" and illiteracy were also shown as deterrents to black stability. Discrimination in trade unions, Du Bois showed, limited black access to better-paying jobs. A "Special Report on Negro Domestic Service in the Seventh Ward" prepared by Isabel Eaton, an M.A. recipient at Fellow of the College Settlements Association, provided copious documentation of the effects of black women's relegation to that vocation: low wages and compensation, negative effects on family and conjugal relations, adverse health effects, savings and expenditure.

Finally, crime and criminality—the subject of several independent speeches and articles by Du Bois in the time of his composition of *The Philadelphia Negro*—came in for heavy scrutiny. This reflected Du Bois's understanding of capitalism's efforts dating to slavery's black Codes—laws passed specifically to punish and restrict the lives of slaves— to police and repress black life. In one of his boldest early statements on the subject, and on U.S. social life generally, Du Bois writes in Chapter XIII, "The Negro Criminal," "Crime is a phenomenon of organized social life, and is the open rebellion of an individual against his social environment."[14] These words could serve as epigraph for numerous urban rebellions against police brutality in black American history, and to outstanding African-American literary works like Richard Wright's 1940 novel *Native Son*.

Simultaneously, Du Bois's perspective in *The Philadelphia Negro* could be moralistic, elitist and idealist, especially towards the black poor and working class. "The lax moral habits of the slave regime still show themselves in a large amount of cohabitation without marriage," he wrote in Chapter VI, "Conjugal Conditions."[15] Single black women, Du Bois argued, were more vulnerable to immoral behavior or prostitution. Conspicuous consumption—untrained spending on superfluous items rather than thrift—plagued the poor. "Money is wasted to-day in dress, furniture, elaborate entertainments, costly church edifices, and 'insurance' schemes, which ought to go towards buying home, educating children . . . and accumulating something in the savings bank for a 'rainy day.'"[16] Black suffrage, Du Bois writes patronizingly, should be given out only to those educated in politics. "Moral weakness" is listed as cause of some black criminality.[17]

Du Bois also prescribes that the "better classes of the Negroes should recognize their duties toward the masses" in the name of Negro reform, while whites must work to reduce racism within their own ranks and "gain their active aid and co-operation" of better class blacks by "generous and polite conduct."[18] Du Bois's paternalist scheme in many ways epitomizes the high point of his nineteenth-century training in bourgeois reformism.

At the same time as he was finishing his work in Philadelphia, Du Bois was undertaking one of the most important new activities of his life. In July, 1900, he attended the first Pan-African Congress in London in July, 1900. The meeting was organized primarily by Henry Sylvester Williams, a Trinidadian barrister who coined the term "Pan-Africa." Williams intended the first Congress to be a rebuke to the colonizing countries, especially Great Britain, for failing to uphold African rights especially in South Africa.[19] Sylvester identified Du Bois to attend the meeting and speak at its closing session largely because of his notoriety in helping to found the Academy of the American Negro and his publication of *The Philadelphia Negro*. Sylvester's idea was to bring together for the first time in one place leading intellectuals of the African diaspora and to create an organization that could combat colonialism and racism. Still, the event's political thrust was reformist, not radical. Of the 33 participants who attended, most were black elites with professional credentials in fields ranging from medicine to music. Du Bois was among six U.S. delegates. Two others were women, the radical reformers Anna Julia Cooper and Ada Harris. Cooper's contribution to the meeting was her paper "The Negro in America" which criticized Christian hypocrisy in a racist America. The meeting was presided over by Bishop Alexander

Walters of the African Methodist Episcopal Zion denomination. Walters was noteworthy for his defense of black voting rights.

Du Bois was motivated to attend the conference by his desire to see the fate of Africa tied to the rest of the world. Though he had done no formal study on the continent, after his Berlin trip and his return to racist America, he was more than ever eager to discuss the problem of what he called the "world color line." David Levering Lewis has rightly characterized the Pan-African Congress in London as "derivative" of other nineteenth-century nationalist movements—Pan-Hellenism, Pan-Germanism, Pan-Slavism—"exploding onto the twentieth century like a stick of dynamite."[20] The Congress represented in other words the chance for people of the African diaspora to see themselves as part of the same racial and national group. On July 23, 24, 25, 1900, delegates to the Congress met in Westminster Town Hall. The most lasting political theme of the meeting was provided by Du Bois. His "To the Nations of the World" speech, delivered at the closing session of the Congress, endeavored to use "civilizationist" discourse of the previous century to temper, erode and potentially abolish colonialism in the coming one. Arguing that "the darker races are to-day the least advanced in culture according to European standards," Du Bois wrote:

> If now the world of culture bends itself towards giving Negroes and other dark men the largest and broadest opportunity for education and self-development, then this contact and influence is bound to have a beneficial effect upon the world and hasten human progress. But if, by reason of carelessness, prejudice, greed and injustice, the black world is to be exploited and ravished and degraded, the results must be deplorable, if not fatal, not simply to them, but to the high ideals of justice, freedom and culture which a thousand years of Christian civilization have held before Europe.[21]

Du Bois followed with a set of demands couched in the language of humanistic idealism: "Let not mere colour or race be a feature of distinction drawn between white and black men, regardless of worth or ability;" "Let not the natives of Africa be sacrificed to the greed of gold . . ."; "Let not the cloak of Christian missionary enterprise be allowed in the future, as so often in the past, to hide the ruthless economic exploitation and political downfall of less developed nation;" "Let the German Empire and the French Republic, true to their great past, remember that the true worth of colonies lies in their prosperity and progress, and that justice, impartial alike to black and white, is the first element of prosperity." And then finally this *magna carta* for global black sovereignty:

> Let the nations of the World respect the integrity and independence of the free Negro states of Abyssinia, Liberia, Hayti, etc., and let the inhabitants of these States, the independent tribes of Africa, the Negroes of the West Indies and America, and the black subjects of all nations take courage, strive ceaselessly, and fight bravely, that they may prove to the world their incontestable right to be counted among the great brotherhood of mankind.[22]

Where *The Philadelphia Negro* called for black and white elites to collaborate in social reform to improve black lives, "To the Nations of the World" pleaded with the leading capitalist and colonial countries of the West to recognize the rights and full humanity of people of African descent. The Congress's program might be called progressive anti-racist humanism. But the analysis of colonialism and its "ruthless economic exploitation" also showed Du Bois's education in Socialist perspective begun in Germany. "To the Nations of the World" is also important for being the first time in his writing that Du Bois would use the famous sentence "The problem of the twentieth century is the problem of the color line."

What was the influence and effect of the 1900 Pan-African Congress? In general, quite limited. Only 33 persons participated, few from Africa, thus limiting the real and political reach of the conference. Because the goals of the meeting were reformist, its objectives did not upset mainstream imperialism in the least. Disorganization was also a problem. Williams died young at age 42 and never organized a follow-up meeting in his lifetime. Du Bois returned to America and threw himself into the formation of domestic civil rights organizations. The logistics of an international gathering across continents also made follow-up meetings difficult. Because elites constituted the Congress, they had virtually no ties to working-class movements or the organized left, like the Socialist movements, hence were marginalized to labor upturns in North American, Europe and Africa between 1900 and the beginning of World War I. Put another way, the Congress had no practical orientation to the labor question. Thus it wasn't until 1919 that the Second Pan-African Congress was held, in Paris, this one motivated by the end of World War I and the plight of the colonies under the Treaty of Versailles. By that time the Bolshevik Revolution, the development of Communist parties across the world, and the leftward turn of African and Caribbean diasporic intellectuals would give the work of the Congress a more militant cast, as we will discuss later. However, in context, the 1900 Congress should be seen as something of a missed opportunity for sustained collaboration and leadership in the battle against colonialism and imperialism.

Du Bois spent 13 years before and after the London Pan-African Congress, from 1897 to 1910, as a faculty member at Atlanta University, another African-American university created after emancipation. Here his main contribution was "the development at an American institution of higher learning, of a program of study on the problems affecting the American Negroes, covering a progressively widening and deepening effort designed to stretch over the span of a century."[23] Du Bois did systematic study of economic co-operation among African-Americans, small, paid studies for the United States Commissioners of Labor, and a study of Lowndes County, Alabama, a former slave state with a black majority. As Aldon Morris has argued, Du Bois was trying to create something like the first comprehensive sociology of post-emancipation black southern life. His research produced scholarly articles published in academic journals and progressive newspapers mainly in the north, and several articles for the prestigious liberal periodical *The Atlantic Monthly* which were to become chapters in Du Bois's most famous and soon to be published book, *The Souls of Black Folk*. Among these were "Strivings of the Negro People," published in the August 1897 *Atlantic*, and "A Negro Schoolmaster in the New South," also published in the January 1899 *Atlantic*.

The Souls of Black Folk has rightly been canonized as the most influential of Du Bois's books. It was so immediately well received that the German sociologist Max Weber wanted to translate it into German. The book is a multidisciplinary manifesto on race segregation, racial oppression, African-American history, and the historical wounds and strivings of African-Americans. A holistic accounting of the book demands a dialectic mode of reading.

In "The Forethought," a brief preamble to the book, Du Bois repeats a sentence from "To the Nations of the World" to indicate that *Souls* should take its place as a sequel to, and constituent part of, Pan-Africanism: "the problem of the Twentieth Century is the problem of the color-line." Du Bois also introduces one of his most famous and persistent tropes in "The Forethought." This is the "Veil" through which African-Americans see the world. The veil is imagined as both a partition between the "two worlds"—black and white—and a looking glass or standpoint from which to articulate black consciousness and a critique of the dominant society. This idea is most famously articulated within a version of the "civilizationist" framework we have visited in Du Bois's earlier writings:

> After the Egyptian and Indian, the Greek and Roman, the Teuton and Mongolian, the Negro is a sort of seventh son, born with a veil, and gifted with second-sight in this American world,—a world which yields him no true self-consciousness, but only lets him see himself through the revelation of the other world. It is a peculiar sensation, this double- consciousness, this sense of always looking at one's self through the eyes of others, of measuring one's soul by the tape of a world that looks on in amused contempt and pity. One ever feels his twoness,—an American, a Negro; two souls, two thoughts, two unreconciled strivings; two warring ideals in one dark body, whose dogged strength alone keeps it from being torn asunder.[24]

Du Bois's theory of alienation here, like Marx's, presumes historical oppression, or "social being" as determinant of consciousness. "Double consciousness" is the psychological expression of Jim Crow reality in America, literally the manifestation of social and political segregation. Du Bois also indicates what Eric Porter calls his "disidentificatory Americanism" in this passage. The "Negro" is a civilization apart, and an epistemological "outsider" to the nation and national consciousness. "One ever feels his twoness,—an American, a Negro." Here we see a foreshadow of Du Bois's eventual alienation and exile from America.

Yet at the time of publication, Du Bois's "color line" was primarily the domestic one, his ambition still one of "fostering and developing the traits of the Negro, not in opposition to or contempt for other races, but rather in large conformity to the ideals of the American Republic, in order that some day on American soil two world-races may give to each those characteristics both so sadly lack."[25] That is to say, *The Souls of Black Folk* is a work of racial uplift and reform. Chapter II, "Of the Dawn of Freedom," recounts the 1865 formation by the federal U.S. government of the "Freedmen's Bureau" during Reconstruction intended to assist former slaves at Civil War's end. The Bureau provided medical care to half a million patients, helped establish African-Americans as "peasant proprietors," and established "free schools" offering free elementary education. Du Bois invokes this moment in history as a "dawn of freedom" both to indicate the end of slavery and to signal African-American participation in "self-emancipation" through their work as farmers, educators, bankers, and politicians.

Chapter III, "Of Booker T. Washington and Others," mentioned earlier, shows Du Bois separating himself from the strictly pro-capitalist wing of racial uplift at the turn of the century led by Booker T. Washington. A former slave and founder of the Tuskegee Institute, a black university, Washington exhorted African-Americans to learn a vocation or trade in order to integrate peaceably from the bottom of society, to become "as one finger on the hand" of America. Washington's 1895 "Atlanta Exposition" address calling for African-Americans to pull themselves up by their "bootstraps" remains the most famous formulation of these ideas. For Du Bois, Washington's program was undertaken at the cost of abandoning demands for civil rights and failing to challenge Jim Crow. As Du Bois puts it, Washington asks African-Americans to forfeit "political power," "insistence on civil rights," and "higher education" besides industrial education." Du Bois argued instead that "By every civilized and peaceful method we must strive for the rights which the world accords to men."[26] In comparison to Washington, Du Bois was sounding a note of civil rights militancy. Du Bois would later in his *Autobiography* modify his criticism of Washington and emphasize that both were fighting for racial justice.

Another signal theme of *The Souls of Black Folk* is the legacy of slavery. Chapter IV, "The Meaning of Progress," and Chapter V, "Of the Wings of Atalanta," are tributes to the cradle of African-American civilization, the "Black Belt" American South that was the heart of the plantation cotton industry. Atlanta, for example, was the capital of the state of Georgia during slavery, with one of the largest populations of black people in America. Now a modernizing southern city after emancipation, Atlanta becomes for Du Bois a symbol of "Truth, Beauty, and Goodness." Du Bois also cautions African-Americans not to lower their sights after emancipation to a "question of cash and a lust for gold."[27] Rather, "The need of the South is knowledge and culture"[28]—this is the post-emancipation "soul" of black folk. These two chapters anticipate Du Bois's efforts in Chapters VII and VIII of the book to raise the South, the "Egypt of the confederacy" to a place of black economic production and self-development. Chapter VIII's title "Of the Quest of the Golden Fleece," alludes to the classical hero Jason's mythological quest to dramatize this theme. The essay should be read as companion to Du Bois's 1911 novel *The Quest of the Silver Fleece*, where Du Bois created the fictional character of Zora Cresswell, the daughter of a slave and sharecropper seeking to buy and tender her own land. Her aspiration, or "quest" is a means of rising "up from slavery" and an allegory for a program of southern black economic uplift. The four chapters in *The Souls of Black Folk* on the South also provide a combination of detailed economic data on southern tenant farmers and agriculture as a means to dispel blame and stigmatization of their plight. Du Bois admonishes the "car-window sociologist" who would deem the poor and disenfranchised southerner "Shiftless".[29]

The Souls of Black Folk also uses elements of Du Bois's life story. Chapter XI, "Of the Passing of the First-Born," describes Du Bois's reaction to the death of his son at the age of two in May of 1899. After remembering the "soft, voluptuous roll which the blood of Africa had moulded into his features," the boy's death is described as a symbolic death of the African-American race. "And thus in the

W.E.B. Du Bois, son Burghardt, wife Nina, 1898. W.E.B. Du Bois Papers (MS 312). Burghardt died aged two in 1899. Special Collections and University Archives, University of Massachusetts Amherst Libraries

Land of the Color-Line I saw, as it fell across my baby, the shadow of the Veil."[30] The elegiac essay foreshadows the last highly personal essay in the book, "The Sorrow Songs," Du Bois's meditation on the multiple meanings and legacies of African-American music. Du Bois recalls hearing for the first time gospel and spirituals in Nashville on his first trip south. He deems "the Negro folk-song—the rhythmic cry of the slave" as "the sole American music" and "the most beautiful expression of human experience born this side the seas." Like the Negro, however, the music has been "neglected" and " half-despised" though it remains "the singular spiritual heritage of the nation and the greatest gift of the Negro people."[31] Du Bois ends *The Souls of Black Folk* with an appeal to the reader to recognize both African-Americans and African culture as essential to western civilization.

The Souls of Black Folk is both monumental and overestimated among Du Bois's works. Its theme of the "color line" or racism as a social institution and its penetrating conception of "double consciousness" have become key concepts in the language of race in

America. The book also shows the early influence of Du Bois's German education. As David Levering Lewis writes, "The German influences are unmistakable with their suggestions of materializing spirit and dialectical struggle, the whole surging process come to concretion in das Volk—a mighty nation with a unique soul."[32] However, many scholars and lay readers end their education in Du Bois with this one book. Du Bois published it at age 35, but lived and wrote until 95. As we shall see, within five years Du Bois was reformulating many of his own ideas about race, racism, capitalism, and the relationship between scholarship and activism. The book is most important, then, as a synthesis of the reformist period of his thought, and as a breakthrough in scholarship on African-Americans. The book should also be re-read and reinterpreted against the large body of work Du Bois produced after it which self-consciously revised its ideas.

3

Socialism, Activism, and World War I

In 1905, the Japanese Army defeated the Tsar's Russian forces in an inter-imperial territorial war over Manchuria, China. From his home in the Jim Crow U.S., Du Bois assessed the event as the first great victory by a "colored" nation over a white one. "The magic of the word 'white' is already broken, and the Color Line in civilization has been crossed in modern times as it was in the great past. The awakening of the yellow races is certain. That the awakening of the brown and black races will follow in time, no unprejudiced student of history can doubt."[1] Russia's military defeat also galvanized the confidence of young Russian revolutionaries, led by V.I. Lenin, who in 1905 attempted, and failed, Russia's first revolution.

At the same time, Du Bois was frustrated with the lack of militant black leadership at home in the U.S. Booker T. Washington, founder of the Tuskegee Institute in Alabama, and an ex-slave, had become the unofficial spokesperson for African-Americans in the eyes of white America. Washington earned the favor of U.S. President Theodore Roosevelt by advocating for black self-help and subordinating demands for civil rights. Du Bois felt that Washington's calls for integration came at the cost of legal and economic protections for black people.

These events in combination jumpstarted Du Bois's gradual turn from reformer to revolutionary. In 1905, he joined with "Fifty-nine colored men from 17 different states" near Niagara Falls, New York, in 1905 to form the "Niagara Movement." Co-leader in the founding of Niagara was William Trotter. Born in Ohio, Trotter graduated from Harvard and thereafter founded the *Boston Guardian* newspaper. In 1905, the same year as the founding of Niagara, he originated the Negro Suffrage League. Trotter was an ardent opponent of segregation. He was temperamental but tenacious and politically closely aligned with Du Bois's views of what Niagara could become. Other players in the formation of Niagara were Harry Clay Smith, editor of the *Cleveland Gazette*, and several friends of Du Bois, young, educated college graduates dedicated to Du Bois's general conception of the "Talented Tenth."

Though founded by elites, Niagara's platform was meant to be a militant alternative to Booker T. Washington's advocacy of "bootstrap capitalism" for African-Americans. Born into slavery, and a graduate of Hampton Institute, one of the black colleges established after emancipation, Washington had emerged as a major figure in black politics in 1881 when he co-founded the Tuskegee Normal School for Colored Teachers in Tuskegee, Alabama, later the Tuskegee Normal and Industrial Institute. In September 1895, Washington delivered what is known as the "Atlanta Exposition Address," encouraging African-Americans to "cast down their buckets" in vocational training while subordinating demands for civil and political rights. As Washington famously put in the speech, "In all things that are purely social we can be as separate as the fingers, yet one as the hand in all things essential to mutual progress." The speech inaugurated what became known as Washington's "Atlanta compromise." In 1901, Washington published his autobiography, *Up From Slavery*, in which he modeled black upward mobility and entrepreneurship as a strategy for the post-emancipation era. Washington became known as administrator of the "Tuskegee Machine," a political lobbying and patronage group that successfully, and compliantly, worked with white industrialists and white elected officials to forward his uplift mission. In *The Souls of Black Folk* and elsewhere, Du Bois savaged Washington and his program for offering to "kiss the hands that smite us."[2] Washington, Du Bois charged, was abandoning three critical aspects of black freedom struggle: civil rights, political power, and higher education. He also argued that without suffrage, black economic upward mobility would be entirely constrained, and that Washington's concessions to white power would shift the burden of racial uplift entirely onto black shoulders. Finally, Washington's narrow orientation to black economic activity was savaged by Du Bois as a "gospel of Work and Money."

All of the signatories to the Niagara movement considered themselves staunch opponents of Washingtonian ideology and Washingtonian strategies for racial justice. The "split" between Washington and Niagara thus constituted the first major fracture in African-American reformism of the twentieth century, one side leaning to assimilation and accommodation, the other to direct action protest and black self-determination. In 1906, the Niagara Movement published the two-page leaflet titled "Address to the Country" indirectly but implicitly targeting Washington and the Tuskegee Machine: "Step by step the defenders of the rights of American citizens have retreated."[3] "Against this the Niagara Movement eternally protests. We will not be satisfied to take one jot or tittle less than our full manhood rights."[4]

Niagara's eight founding principles included "Manhood suffrage," "A belief in the dignity of labor" and "The abolition of all caste distinction based simply on race and color."[5] It also called for enforcement of the law "against rich as well as poor," education for black children, and improvement in schools for African-American children. "These are some of the chief things we want," the address intoned. "How shall we get them? By voting where we may vote, by persistent, unceasing agitation; by hammering at the truth, by sacrifice and work."[6]

The Niagara Movement's militant aspirations were symbolized by its meeting at Harper's Ferry, Virginia, site of abolitionist John Brown's 1859 armed attack on a U.S. arsenal meant to place guns in the hands of his 22 fellow fighters, black and white, to undertake the liberation of plantation slaves. "And here on the scene of John Brown's martyrdom we reconsecrate ourselves, our honor, our property, to the final emancipation of the race which John Brown died to make free." Brown's plan, capture and execution by the federal government motivated Du Bois's 1909 biography *John Brown*. The book inspired Du Bois to write the first part of the epigraph to this book—"Revolution is not a test of capacity." Brown was a hero to Du Bois because of his uncompromising commitment to fighting racism and his bravery in working across the "color line" to try and end it. As had the Niagara Movement document, Du Bois praised Brown not for his strategies of violent armed rebellion but for embodying the spirit of resistance to black oppression. "Of all inspiration which America owes to Africa, however; the greatest by far is the score of heroic men whom the sorrows of these dark children called to unselfish devotion and heroic self-realization,"[7] including Abraham Lincoln, Frederick Douglass, and Brown himself. In 1962, not long before his death, Du Bois would revise the text of his 1909 book for a Soviet edition which would also align Brown's revolutionary determination with the Bolshevik Revolution of 1917 and the Chinese Revolution of 1949. Where in the original 1909 edition Du Bois referred to revolution as a "lowering of ideals," his revision added this sentence: "But if it is a true revolution it repays all losses and results in the uplift of the human race." The revision was consistent with Du Bois's late-in-life efforts to endorse revolutionary struggle against racism and capitalism even if that struggle demanded the use of armed struggle.

Indeed, Du Bois's turn to activism was also a response to continuing racist violence on American soil. From September 22–24, 1906, whites attacked and killed dozens of African-Americans in an event known as the "Atlanta Race Riots." Du Bois would write a poem about the event, "The Litany of Atlanta" and an article titled "Atlanta's Shame." In August 1908, whites in Springfield, Illinois trying to lynch a black man attacked and killed dozens of other African-Americans. Du Bois now felt he had to do more than just write books and articles. As he wrote, "one could not be a calm, cool, and detached scientist while Negroes were lynched, murdered and starved."[8] In a short time, Du Bois would leave his academic position at Atlanta University, declaring later "My career as a scientist was to be swallowed up in my role as master of propaganda."[9]

Du Bois's new platform for activism was the National Association for the Advancement of Colored People (NAACP), and its political organ, the magazine *The Crisis*. In 1910, Du Bois resigned his position at Atlanta University to become the first Director of Publications and Research for the NAACP. The NAACP was the first mass African-American civil rights organization in the United States. David Levering Lewis has characterized the NAACP as "primarily a white organization dedicated to African-American uplift through well-financed suasion; the second, as an interracial phalanx challenging the mainstream public to accept ever-greater civil and social rights for the nation's historic minority."[10] Its original membership included many former members of the Niagara Group, including William Trotter, and several white members of the Socialist Party of the U.S., including social worker Florence Kelley, William Walling, and Mary White Ovington. Also a founding member was the liberal philanthropist Oswald Garrison Villard, grandson of abolitionist William Lloyd Garrison. The NAACP made public campaigns against lynching a central plank of its work from the outset. For example, a black flag was hung from the high window of its Fifth Avenue New York office each time an African-American was lynched, and the organization regularly lobbied the federal government to pass anti-lynching legislation. The Association's lawyers also lobbied to overturn Jim Crow segregation laws in the South, and helped win the right of African-Americans to serve as officers in World War I. The Association successfully campaigned against President Woodrow Wilson's attempts to introduce segregation into public housing and helped overturn "grandfather clauses" meant to restrict black voting rights in the south. Finally, the NAACP famously organized a national boycott campaign against D.W. Griffith's racist 1915 film *The Birth of a Nation*, which glorified the role of the Ku Klux Klan—a landmark struggle in black fights against racist stereotyping and white supremacy.

Its activities fulfilled Du Bois's hopes that the NAACP would develop a mass, interracial base of support for black civil rights wider than the largely academic and elitist Niagara Movement. Yet from the beginning, there were tensions within the organization and Du Bois's role in it. For example, despite supporting its formation Ida B. Wells-Barnett did not sign on as a founding member of the organization because she was distrustful of working with whites. Du Bois did not consider himself a good manager or fundraiser, tasks the organization Board hoped he might fulfill, but rather saw himself as the intellectual and political spokesperson for the organization. He also bristled at what he considered paternalistic suggestions from those white liberals (like Villard and philanthropist Joel Spingarn) about how to run the organization. Thus Du Bois made *The Crisis* something of a personal mouthpiece where he could guarantee to set the political line of the organization. Working in the position

Cole. Delegates from Junior NAACP, Cleveland, with W.E.B. Du Bois, 1929.
W.E.B. Du Bois Papers (MS 312). Special Collections and University Archives,
University of Massachusetts Amherst Libraries

of Director of Publications and Research, Du Bois conceived *The Crisis* as an instrument to "place . . . before the country a clear-cut statement of the legitimate aims of the American Negro and the facts concerning his condition."[11] He used it to report on lynchings, discrimination against black soldiers during the war, and wrote regular "Opinion" columns generally agitating against racist restrictions. He also turned the magazine into a literary organ, hiring the aspiring and talented Jessie Redmon Fauset, later author of the novel *Plum Bun*, as fiction editor. During the 1920s, *The Crisis* regularly published poetry and fiction that became seminal to the Harlem Renaissance. For example, Langston Hughes's groundbreaking poem "The Negro Speaks of Rivers" was first published in *The Crisis* and helped make Hughes a literary star. By 1920, *The Crisis* had developed into the most important African-American publication in the United States. It began with a circulation of 1,000 but grew by 1918 to more than 100,000 copies.[12]

As part of his radicalizing turn, Du Bois also joined the Socialist Party of the U.S. in 1911, one year after signing on to work with the NAACP. The Socialist Party of the U.S. was founded in 1901. One of its organizers was the railroad worker and union activist Eugene Debs. The founding of the Socialist Party reflected the massive upturn in labor union militancy in the United States after the end of the Civil War in response to the rise of industrial capitalism and the so-called "Gilded Age" of wealth accumulation symbolized by men like railroad tycoon Leland Stanford, steel magnate Andrew Carnegie, oil capitalist John D. Rockefeller, retailer Marshall Field, and James Buchanan Duke (tobacco) nicknamed "robber barons" by working people of their time.

Du Bois was originally drawn to socialism because he felt that racism and capitalism went hand in hand. In "The Negro and Socialism," (1907), for example, Du Bois wrote of African-Americans, "We have been made tools of oppression against the workingman's cause—the puppets and playthings of the idle rich."[13] A solution lay in a "larger ideal of human brotherhood, equality of opportunity and work not for wealth but for Weal."[14] In 1908, he wrote in a letter to C.C. Owens, "I believe the Negro problem is partly the American Caste problem & that caste is arising because of unjust and dangerous economic conditions."[15] By 1911, Du Bois wrote that Socialists "rang truest" on race questions.[16] But the biggest influence on Du Bois's commitment to socialism was Eugene Debs himself. It was Debs's 1903 essay "The Negro and Socialism" that had initially won Du Bois's attention to socialism. Debs was a vehement anti-racist who refused to speak to segregated audiences.

Yet Debs was himself to the left of most his socialist contemporaries in centering the fight against racism. For example, Victor Berger, the first socialist elected to the U.S. House of Representatives, defended segregation and made racist remarks about Chinese and African-Americans. Du Bois himself complained accurately that the Socialist Party refused to challenge Jim Crow in the South by allowing segregated political meetings, and made little effort to recruit black workers.[17] The American Federation of Labor, the dominant craft union in the country, routinely discriminated against black labor in this period; its leader Samuel Gompers was a virulent nativist and often attacked foreign labor as a threat to American workers.[18]

These weaknesses in U.S. socialism and the U.S. labor movement were responsible for Du Bois leaving the Socialist Party in 1912 after only one year. Du Bois's lingering elitism, skepticism about working-class unity, and faith in top-down reforms (like the "Talented Tenth") also led to his most egregious political mistakes: his support for Woodrow Wilson as President in the 1912 election. Du Bois was fooled by Wilson's campaign promises to assist the lives of African-Americans. Wilson was in fact an out and out racist: he supported Jim Crow legislation in the South and attempted to expand it into public policy in the North. Famously, Wilson was a fan of D. W. Griffith's racist epic *Birth of a Nation*: he screened the film at the White House and declared it an example of "history written in lightning." Du Bois almost immediately recanted his support for Wilson after his election and later rued the decision to support him. This moment of political confusion indicates profound limits on Du Bois's interpretation of both socialism and democracy in this period. His decision to join the Socialist Party was a narrow and shallow one tethered more to a desire for race reform than class struggle or a strong attack on capitalism. Like other liberals and even right-wing socialists, Du Bois also believed in this period that "parliamentary reform" and electoral politics might be sufficient to achieve social justice. That is, Du Bois was at best in the pre-war period a liberal social democrat. The apex of this confusion was Du Bois's somewhat notorious 1918 *Crisis* editorial "Close Ranks" in which he appealed to African-Americans to set aside their racial grievances in support of the U.S. effort in World War I. Du Bois's decision might be compared to German Social Democratic Party parliamentarians who (with the exception of Karl Liebnicht) voted to support the Chancellor and war bonds in 1914 during the War. We will return later in this chapter to examine in more depth the usefulness of this analogy.

In 1911, Du Bois took a break from his NAACP duties to attend the first Universal Races Congress in Paris organized by the British wing of the Ethical Culture movement. The Universal Races Congress was a meeting of scholars and researchers trying to bring together the best and newest research and thought on the study of race and racism. English economist John Hobson discussed the role of finance capital in imperialism at the Congress, but Du Bois lamented that the "labor question" and timelines for decolonization of India and Egypt was not addressed.[19] He wanted the meeting to have more concrete political objectives. This was reflected in Du Bois's own contribution to the meeting, the anti-war poem "A Hymn to the Peoples." Du Bois said later that the Congress "would have marked an epoch in the racial history of the world if it had not been for the World War"[20] which broke out three years after the first Congress. Mainly, the failures of the Congress to generate real political gains demonstrated the gap between Du Bois and the world's colored elites and anything like a mass global movement for equality.

World War I was both a shock and a turning point in Du Bois's life. It raised contradictions between his aspirations for racial reforms in the United States and the emergence of the U.S. as an imperialist power. For example, Du Bois initially supported U.S. entry into the war in 1917. He saw the war as a chance for African-Americans to gain further civil rights, consistent with his racial reformist impulses. Under the Selective Service Act, 700,000 African-Americans registered in 1917 to fight for the United States. Du Bois hoped that such a show of national loyalty would be rewarded by the state. As noted above, Du Bois therefore encouraged African-Americans to "close ranks" and set aside racial grievances during the war in the name of national unity.

Yet Du Bois also saw the war between the European powers, and U.S. participation in it, as an attempt to spread western imperialistic reach across the world. In May 1915, in the second year of World War I, Du Bois published the essay "The African Roots of the War" in the widely read liberal periodical *Atlantic Monthly*. The seven-page essay, written when he was 47 years old, begins by reminding readers of Africa's role as a cradle of civilization—"It was through Africa that Christianity became the religion of the world."[21] From there Du Bois moves to analysis of the Berlin Conference of 1884 where colonialism set its violent course: "Lying treaties, rivers of rum, murder, assassination, mutilation, rape, and torture have marked the progress of Englishman, German, Frenchman, and Belgian on the dark continent."[22] The conquest of Africa induced a new world

"Color Line" and an enduring scramble for Africa among European countries "groping toward the new Imperialism."[23]

> Whence comes this new wealth and on what does its accumulation depend? It comes primarily from the darker nations of the world— Asia and Africa, South and Central America, the West Indies and the islands of the South Seas ... Chinese, East Indians, Negroes and South American Indians, are by common consent for governance by white folk and economic subjection to them.[24]

Du Bois here looks backward to Marx's "primitive accumulation" to describe colonialism's new role in building capitalism in the modern world. It is why he refers to Africa as the "Land of the Twentieth Century."[25] Emphasis on imperialism includes his understanding of the modern day United States as an imperialist country, despite its lack of formal "colonial" holdings in Africa. The U.S. for example had annexed Puerto Rico, Cuba, the Philippines and Hawaii in the year 1898.

Du Bois also offers one of his first interpretations in "The African Roots of War" of the relationship between modern capitalism and nationalism. "The present world war is, then, the result of jealousies engendered by the recent rise of armed national associations of labor and capital whose aim is the exploitation of the wealth of the world mainly outside the European circle of nations."[26] Native labor conditions and practices dividing workers by race and nation buttress this imperial order: "By threatening to send English capital to China and Mexico, by threatening to hire Negro laborers in America, as well as by old-age pensions and accident insurance, we gain industrial peace at home at the mightier cost of war abroad."[27] Capitalism then, seeking "to unite labor and capital in world-wide freebooting," admits to a "share of the spoils of capital only the aristocracy of labor— the more intelligent and shrewder and cannier workingmen. The ignorant, unskilled, and restless still form a large, threatening, and to a growing extent, revolutionary group in advanced countries."[28]

Du Bois here assigns the cause of World War I to inter-imperial rivalry, meaning competition between capitalist nations. His use of the phrase "aristocracy of labor" also aligned him with both Engels's argument in *The Condition of the Working Class in England* that English trade unions constituted a labor "aristocracy," and with Lenin's more developed argument in *Imperialism: The Highest Stage of Capitalism*, that a layer of privileged workers bought off by the capitalist class helped to advance the exploitation of non-privileged workers beneath them.[29] Against these conditions Du Bois proposes African diasporic unity and international collaboration between colonized peoples, including African-Americans:

> In this great work who can help us? In the Orient, the awakened Japanese and the awakened leaders of New China; in India and Egypt, the young men trained in Europe and European ideals, who now form the stuff that Revolution is born of. But in Africa? Who better than the twenty-five million grandchildren of the European slave trade, spread through the Americas, and now writing desperately for freedom and a place in the world? And of these millions first of all the ten million Black folk of the United States, now a problem, then a world-salvation.[30]

"The African Roots of the War" is important in several respects. First, it reflected Du Bois's gradual interpretation of twentieth-century wars as wars fought for capital and its ruling classes. Second, Du Bois forever after World War I saw racism and the plight of non-white peoples as central to imperialist rule. This was driven home by the upturn in U.S. lynchings during and after the war, by what Du Bois called the "extraordinary difficulties of the draft and the question of Negro officers" fighting in a segregated U.S. military."[31] There was also the "Red Summer" of 1919, when hundreds of returning African-American soldiers and workers faced new forms of racism spurred by labor competition and xenophobia.

"The African Roots of War" also shows Du Bois shifting gradually but clearly further to the left. Du Bois's analysis of the imperial roots of war, that is, aligned him long-term to the perspective of other revolutionaries (Lenin, Trotsky, Rosa Luxemburg) who broke with the "right" socialists in the Second International, particularly the German Social Democratic Party, who as noted earlier voted for war credits and supported their imperial state in the war. To put this another way, Du Bois's political turn to the left hastened by the war allows us to see his own contradictions reflected in wider left currents of the period. Du Bois's residual nationalism, his liberal integration-ist hopes for African-American participation in democracy, even his faith and confidence in capitalism itself, were all gradually shattered by his eventual recognition of the war as an imperialist attack on the world's working classes—a perspective he did not hold in 1912 or 1914. After World War I, it would be impossible for Du Bois to perceive the U.S. state as an ally either in African-American freedom struggle or for example the liberation of African peoples. Du Bois instead would become a harsh critic of Woodrow Wilson's claim that U.S. participation in the war "made the world safe for democracy."

Indeed the essay "African Roots of the War" was influenced by Du Bois's growing attention to Asian national movements reflected in both the long-term influence of the Japanese victory over Russia in 1905, China's 1911 Republican Revolution, and Du Bois's attendance at the Universal Races Congress of 1911. He was beginning to understand race and racism as global phenomena linked to global capital. Thus we can see Du Bois in this period challenging radicals and socialists to do more for African-Americans. He told participants at the Intercollegiate Socialist Society that "Revolution is discussed but it is the successful revolution of white folk."[32] Socialists had to fight harder for the rights of black workers migrating during the war from the south to the north to take industrial jobs. Du Bois anticipates directives from the Communist International after 1919 that the U.S. Communist Party must take up the special task of fighting for black workers and integrating them into the Communist movement.

Du Bois's turn towards global activism culminated in the years of 1919 and 1920. Du Bois wrote a letter to President Woodrow Wilson insisting that the "International Peace Congress" recognize that within the U.S. resided "twelve million souls whose consent to be governed is never asked. They have no members in the legislatures of states where they are in the majority, and not a single representative in the national congress."[33] In February 1919, Du Bois gathered at the Grand Hotel in Paris 57 delegates to the second official Pan-African Congress. Sixteen African-Americans were among the delegates. Du Bois was hoping to use Wilson's own principles ostensibly supporting the self-determination of nations after the war to push forward the struggle of African nations to become free of colonial rule. Though little emerged from the Congress but resolutions of support for African diasporic self-determination, Du Bois had set the stage for a new period of anti-colonial struggle.

In 1920, Du Bois published his masterpiece of the World War I era, *Darkwater: Voices From Within the Veil*. The book might be called Du Bois's anti-imperialist sequel to *The Souls of Black Folk*. Where *The Souls of Black Folk* served as a manifesto of the domestic "color line" and double-consciousness, *Darkwater* builds upon Du Bois's "African Roots of War" an analysis of the part labor, racism and—a new topic for Du Bois—women's oppression play in combating Western empire. The title of the book is a pun on Lothrop Stoddard's eugenicist-influenced book *The Rising Tide of Color Against White World Supremacy*, published the same year. The racist Stoddard warned that World War I was producing a white holocaust that would shift the tide of human reproduction to the non-white races. The final section of the book includes a poem by Du Bois which is a stern riposte to Rudyard Kipling's famous description of the "white man's burden," written to commemorate U.S. imperial reach into the Caribbean in 1898.

Darkwater starkly describes World War I as slow colonial genocide in need of immediate and radical response: "I believe that War is Murder . . . I believe that the wicked conquest of weaker and darker nations by nations whiter and stronger but foreshadows the death of that strength."[34] The book's third essay, "The Hands of Ethiopia," is an updated and revised version of Du Bois's "African Roots of War," emboldened by the end of war and Du Bois's 1919 Pan-African Congress to a new declaration of African self-determination:

. . . let us set the conception of a new African World State, a Black Africa, applying to these peoples the splendid pronouncements which have of late been so broadly and perhaps carelessly given the world: recognizing in Africa the declaration of the American Federation of Labor, that 'no people must be forced under sovereignty under which it does not wish to live'; recognizing in President Wilson's message to the Russians, the 'principle of the undictated development of all peoples';[35]

Du Bois's reference to the notoriously racist American Federation of Labor underscores the necessity for black labor—and interracial labor unity—to combat racism and imperialism. Chapter IV of the book, "Of Work and Wealth," focuses on East St. Louis, Missouri, where in the summer of 1919, newly industrialized black workers were attacked in deadly race riots by white workers returning from war to new labor competition for their old jobs. Du Bois describes St. Louis as a microcosm of wartime accumulation for capital, and black workers as the new "exploited" alongside white workers whose successful attempts at strikes for higher wages were undone by union discrimination, driving 5,000 black workers from the city. Du Bois describes this black pogrom as a world-historical loss:

It was the old world horror come to life again; all that Jews suffered in Spain and Poland; all that peasants suffered in France, and Indians in Calcutta; all that aroused human deviltry had accomplished in ages past they did in East St. Louis, where the rags of six thousand half-naked black men and women fluttered across the bridges of the calm Mississippi.[36]

Du Bois poses proletarian unity as a necessary step against industrial tyranny: "What I had to show was that no real organization of industry could be permanently made with the majority of mankind left out. These disinherited darker peoples must either share in the future industrial democracy or overturn the world."[37]

Darkwater also featured Du Bois's first published essay on women's oppression. "The Damnation of Women" analyzes women's role under capitalism in the social reproduction of labor and profits. "The world wants healthy babies and intelligent workers . . . Only at the sacrifice of intelligence and the chance to do their best work can the majority of modern women bear children. This is the damnation of women."[38] From this material base flow sexist ideologies: "All womanhood is hampered today because the world on which it is emerging is a world that tries to workshop both virgins and mothers and in the end despises motherhood and despoils virgins."[39] Du Bois's essay reflects the spirit of both contemporary suffragist feminism (he advocated women's right to vote and birth control) and the demands of socialist feminism emerging in the writings of contemporaries like Charlotte Perkins Gilman in the U.S. (whom he cites in the essay) and Clara Zetkin in Germany.

The specific role of black women in the reproduction, and social reproduction, of slavery and capitalism is Du Bois's chief subject in the essay. "The crushing weight of slavery fell on black women" he writes. "Under it there was no legal marriage, no legal family, no legal control over children."[40] Black women were instead, quoting his mentor, the historian Alexander Crummell, "mated as the stock of the plantation were mated, not to be the companion of a loved and chosen husband, but to be the breeder of human cattle for the field or the auction block."[41] Black women were further subject to rape, shame, and sexual stereotype: "her chivalrous and whiter mate could caste her off at his pleasure and publicly sneer at the body he had privately blasphemed."[42]

The legacy of slavery for black women is also condemned in the essay. Under contemporary capitalism, Du Bois argues, black women play a critical role in the labor forces as domestics, washerwomen, teachers disproportionate to white women. "There were in 1910 two and a half million Negro homes in the United States. Out of these homes walked daily to work two million women and girls over ten years of age—over half of the colored population as against a fifth in the case of white women."[43] Thus women's, and black women's, specific historical experience of exploitation and oppression must become central to any analysis of capitalism:

Indeed, here, in microcosm and with differences emphasizing sex equality, is the industrial history of labor in the 19th and 20th centuries. We cannot abolish the new economic freedom of women. We cannot imprison women again in a home or require them all on pain of death to be nurses and housekeepers.

What is today the message of these black women to America and to the world? The uplift of women is, next to the problem of the color line and the peace movement, our greatest modern cause. When, now, two of these movements—woman and color—combine in one, the combination has deep meaning."[44]

Du Bois here speaks to what black Communists like Louise Patterson and Claudia Jones would later call black women's "triple exploitation" under capitalism—as workers, as women, as African-Americans. Du Bois's 1911 novel *The Quest of the Silver Fleece* addressed these themes through the life of Zora Cresswell. Cresswell is a young, female entrepreneur attempting to rise "up from slavery." She struggles to attain control of both land and her body in a society which disenfranchises and often rapes black women. Throughout his career, Du Bois was alternately paternalistic and essentialist in his contemplation of sex and gender, and presciently radical. "The Damnation of Women" stands out as a singular moment in his thinking that begs for more theoretical contribution and intervention by the author which he unfortunately never delivered.

In later life, Du Bois said the early years of his intellectual development "followed sociology as the path to social reform and social uplift as a result of scientific investigation."[45] Between the first Pan-African Congress and the end of World War I, Du Bois could be considered a reformist moving slowly in the direction of becoming a revolutionary. Gradual changes in this thinking are seen in "The African Roots of War" and "Of Wealth and Labor," from *Darkwater*. Political revolutions and sharpened economic sufferings by African-Americans would continue to propel Du Bois's thought forward, and take him increasingly outside of the United States to develop an analysis of world events and political strategies for responding to them. These currents will be the focus of the next section of this book.

PART II

FROM MOSCOW TO MANCHESTER, 1917–45

4

Du Bois and
the Russian Revolution

In his unpublished manuscript "Russia and America: An Interpretation" (1950), W.E.B. Du Bois traced his interest in Russia to its 1905 war with Japan and its first failed revolution (1905–07). Both events prompted Du Bois to begin a comparative study between the conditions of peasants under the Tsar and American slaves of the nineteenth century. This research showed Du Bois's first interest in understanding the historical development of capitalism on a global scale. It also indicates Du Bois's first attempt to understand the idea of Socialism as an alternative to capitalism. By the time of the successful Bolshevik Russia of 1917, Du Bois had come to perceive the Russian Revolution, and the experiment of world Communism, as one of the most important events of the twentieth century, and his own development as a political revolutionary. As he later said of the 1917 Bolshevik victory, "It explained me."[1]

This aspect of Du Bois's intellectual and biographical development is the one most overlooked by scholars. Typically, Du Bois's embrace of Communism is treated as a late-in-life development brought about by a strong reaction against Cold War anti-Communism and persecution of radical black intellectuals (like his friend Paul Robeson), a romantic infatuation with Mao's China, or a desperate blindness to the brutalities of Stalinism for which Du Bois was, quite often, either public apologist, or ardent defender. Exceptions to this narrative in Du Bois studies include Du Bois archivist Herbert Aptheker, political biographers Gerald Horne and Manning Marable, and political theorist Cedric Robinson. Each has struggled to interpret contradictions in Du Bois's relationship to Marxism generally. Aptheker, a long-time self-identified Communist, likely influenced

Du Bois's decision in the 1950s to identify himself politically with the Party. Horne sees Du Bois as an idealistic anti-racist and anti-capitalist who was a victim of McCarthyite prosecution during the Cold War. Robinson has usefully recognized the influence of the Russian Revolution and peasant movements on classic Du Bois books like *Black Reconstruction*. Marable meanwhile has coined the term "radical democrat" to describe Du Bois's shifting political perspective, generally lamenting his turn to Stalinist sympathies late in his career.[2]

These interpretations give us partial help in explaining Du Bois's lifelong interest in socialism, Communism, the writings of Karl Mark and Frederich Engels, and his endeavor to develop an analysis and application of Marxist thought. Generally speaking, Du Bois's development as a socialist was marked by uneven theoretical understanding of Marxist ideas, and an orientation to reformism that was characteristic of both his training in U.S. liberalism, early Pan-Africanism, and the Second International Socialism that was concurrent with his move to the left. We have already noted for example Du Bois's attendance at Social Democratic Party meetings in Berlin during his stay as a student. We have also seen his positive reaction as early as 1902 (Du Bois was 34 years of age then) to U.S. socialists like Eugene Debs, who centered the fight against racism in the development of an American socialist tradition. Du Bois also had close friends early in life who persuaded him to become a socialist. In 1908, Du Bois's friend William Walling published the book *Russia's Message: The True World Import of the Revolution*. Reporting back from the first revolution of 1905, Walling sided clearly with Lenin and the Bolsheviks against the Mensheviks, referring to Lenin as "perhaps the most popular leader in Russia."[3] and advocating for "peasant socialism" and the *narod*—workers and peasants—as the revolutionary layer most likely to succeed in an eventual overthrow of Russian feudalism. Though Walling ultimately sided with the Socialist Revolutionary Party over the Bolsheviks in the revolution, and wrote later works disparaging Sovietism, his early attention to the revolution and the role of the peasantry was influential of Du Bois's own, as was his later hesitation about supporting Bolshevism outright. Walling's example also motivated Du Bois to provide his own comparative framework especially between African-Americans and other oppressed national groups. As he wrote after his first visit there, "I can interpret the Soviet Union today through my experience with two million American Negroes in the last half of the nineteenth century."[4]

Indeed, Du Bois's short-lived membership in the Socialist Party expressed his hope that socialism could advance America's own worker and peasant society, groups disproportionately in 1905 African-American. Du Bois's joint research into the conditions of black urban proletariat life in *The Philadelphia Negro* combined with his series of economic studies of black southern agrarian economy at Atlanta University before his 1909 resignation had given him a 'materialist' base by which to analyze the class structure of U.S capitalism and the role of racism in subordinating black workers. In 1925, Du Bois would refer to "the Color Problem and the Labor Problem to so great an extent two sides of the same human tangle."[5]

Thus to understand fully the effect of Russia's 1917 revolution on Du Bois's life and thought we must move methodically through the period of his life between World War I, the time of publication of his important essay "African Roots of the War," and the onset of the global capitalist depression of 1929. These events steered Du Bois permanently and irrevocably in the direction of a Marxist analysis of society, and to an understanding of race and racism as products of capitalism.

Of special significance to his development was the formation of the Communist International (or Comintern) in 1919. The Bolshevik organization dedicated to building a world communist movement took up a question central to Du Bois as a Pan-Africanist, namely the fate of the colonies. Du Bois would be won generally to the Communist International's advocacy of national self-determination both as a formula for decolonization of the non-white world and for African-Americans fighting domestic racism from within the borders of U.S. imperialism. After the Russian Revolution especially, Du Bois was eager to connect more directly the fight for African decolonization to African-American national liberation and economic equality. It was the relationship between the two which compelled Du Bois to argue in 1952, "I believe in Communism wherever and whenever men are wise and good enough to achieve it; but I do not believe all nations will achieve it in the same way or at the same time."[6]

Du Bois was largely self-trained in Marxism and Socialism. As a student at Fisk and Harvard, he was never introduced to Socialist thought. Later in life, Du Bois admitted he was unprepared at first as to how to respond to the first reports of Bolshevism: "I was bewildered at what was happening . . . I certainly believed Russia needed radical reform and was encouraged at the Menshevik effort under Karensky [sic]. When the Bolsheviks came to power, I hesitated: Was this the Thermidor or something more permanent and fundamental? Was Marxian Communism possible or a wild, perverted dream?"[7]

Du Bois's fear about "Thermidor"—the period of violent crackdown and killings of the Jacobins which ended the radical phase of the French Revolution—owed to an orientation to non-violence as reflected in the Niagara movement endorsement of the principles, if not the tactics, of John Brown. Du Bois's worries about the role of force and violence in a worker takeover of state power was also borne from anxiety about racism in the U.S. labor movement. Du Bois feared that racist white workers would not admit black workers as equals even in the name of revolution or that white workers might turn on black workers outright during a revolution. For example, in the 1930s he criticized the Communist Party for trying to use black workers as what he called "shock troops" in an attempt to build an anti-capitalist movement in the South. This impeded his embrace of Leninist doctrines like the need for workers to seize state control of state power, as expressed in his essay "State and Revolution," and temporarily led Du Bois into endorsing as capitalist alternatives black economic cooperatives, as we shall discuss momentarily.

Yet by 1919, Du Bois was emboldened by two events to reassess the need for a workers' revolution. The first was the violence inflicted on black workers during the so-called "Red Summer" of 1919, when racist mobs in Chicago and East St. Louis set upon African-Americans. Labor competition spurred by the return of large number of white workers from World War I was one impetus for the attacks. The assaults deepened Du Bois's animus for capitalism and his concern for the plight of non-white workers worldwide. The second event was the tantalizing early success of the Bolsheviks in creating a society based on workers control. In the September 1919 *Crisis*, for example, in an essay titled "Let's Reason Together," Du Bois linked these two developments. "In this fight for Justice in Labor the negro looms large. In Africa and the South Seas, in all the Americas and dimly in Asia, he is a mighty worker and, potentially perhaps, the mightiest." Seeking to address "The most stupendous labor problem of the twentieth century . . . the problem of Equality of Humanity in the world as against white domination of black and brown and yellow serfs," Du Bois went on:

> The one new Idea of the World War—the one which may well stand in future years as the one thing that made the slaughter worthwhile—is an Idea which we are like to fail to know because it is today hidden under the maledictions hurled at Bolshevism. It is not the murder, the anarchy, the hate which for years under Czar and Revolution have drenched this weary land, but it is the vision of great dreams that only those who work shall vote and rule.[8]

For the first time Du Bois was trying to see through the smoke of the October Revolution a clear path forward for the world's working classes, especially those of what might be called today the "global south." Du Bois was also moved, even pushed, to closer consideration of the Russian Revolution by his black contemporaries, many of whom embraced Communism and the revolution before he did. In 1917, A. Phillip Randolph and Owen Chandler, both members of the Socialist Party which opposed U.S. participation in World War I, started the newspaper *The Messenger*, and leveled public criticism at Du Bois for supporting the war. As they put it in an editorial directed partly at Du Bois, "Our aim is to appeal to reason to lift our pens above the cheap, peanut politics of the old, reactionary Negro leadership."[9] The stinging rhetoric indicated a generational attack by upstarts determined to define what Alain Locke called in 1925 the "new negro" as a more militant alternative to the "old negro." Their challenge to figures like Du Bois, 49 at the time of the Russian Revolution, was clear: embrace radical change or get out of the way. Du Bois initially rebuffed these criticisms, but continued to himself move leftward.

In 1919, the Caribbean radical immigrant and Socialist Party member Hubert Harrison also criticized Du Bois for his "Close Ranks" editorial asking African-Americans to set aside their racial grievances in the name of wartime unity, contending that Du Bois was more interested in currying favor with the state than squarely facing the imperialist, and racist, nature of the war. Harrison had been a member and leading voice against racism of the Socialist Party, founded an important black newspaper called *The Voice*, and served as editor of *The World*, the newspaper of Marcus Garvey's Universal Negro Improvement Association (UNIA). Harrison and Garvey's orientation to see working-class African-American and Caribbean citizens of the U.S. as a revolutionary force was itself a challenge to Du Bois's own more academic and elitist orientation. Du Bois's criticism of Garveyism for being utopian in outlook (Garvey's support for repatriation to Liberia for example) was at the same time symptomatic of a real challenge from the UNIA to develop an economic strategy for the poorest of the black poor in America. Much later, Du Bois would admit that he was too critical of Garvey. Similarly in 1919, Cyril Briggs, a Caribbean immigrant to the U.S., founded the African Blood Brotherhood in New York. The Brotherhood mixed Communism and Pan-Africanism, eventually becoming a propaganda wing of the Communist Party after its founding in 1921. Its center of operations was New York City, not far from Du Bois's NAACP. Its presence guaranteed pressure from the left on Du Bois's organization and his own ideas.

Perhaps the best example of the early radical left influence on Du Bois may be seen in his relationship to the Jamaican poet Claude McKay. McKay, who wrote one of the greatest political protest poems in U.S. history inspired by the "Red Summer" of 1919, "If We Must Die," was invited by the Communist International to Moscow to speak on the conditions of black people in America. The invitation was part of the Comintern's endeavor after 1917 to develop an analysis of the conditions of African-Americans in America which led to its pressuring the U.S. Communist Party to address racism and fight "chauvinism" within the organization. In Moscow, McKay testified that black Americans and immigrants of Caribbean descent faced racist oppression unlike that faced by white and other workers.

McKay penned a short book on the topic, *Negri v. Ameriki* (*The Negro in America*), that was published in Moscow. McKay's testimony, and the book, combined with similar testimonials from figures like American Communist Harry Haywood, spurred the eventual development of the so-called "Black Belt Thesis" at the 1928 Comintern. The thesis argued that African-Americans were an oppressed national minority and maintained a right to secession and independence. The "Black Belt" referred to the southern slaveholding states where African-Americans constituted a significant or majority portion of the population. In effect, the Comintern analogized African-Americans in the U.S. to ethnic national minorities like Georgians and Ukrainians in the former Russia who the Bolsheviks sought to unify by appealing to national self-determination as a step towards proletarian internationalism.

Du Bois invited McKay to write for *The Crisis* after the latter arrived in the Soviet Union to express his views about the Bolshevik revolution. He provided a report in 1922. In December, 1923, McKay published the essay "Soviet Russia and the Negro" in *The Crisis*, which argued that "the Negro, as the most suppressed and persecuted minority, should use this period of ferment in international affairs to lift his cause out of this national obscurity and force it forward as a prime international issue."[10] But Du Bois was slow to change his views as reflected in this 1921 editorial in the NAACP house journal: "Time may prove . . . that the Russian Revolution is the greatest event of the nineteenth and twentieth centuries, and its leaders the most unselfish prophets. At the same time, *The Crisis* does not know this to be true." Because he was still skeptical about racism in the U.S. labor movement, Du Bois also wrote, "How far can the colored people of the world, and particularly the Negroes of the United States, trust the whole working classes?" To this problem Du Bois offered the following solution: "We have to convince the working classes of the world that black men, brown men, and yellow men are human beings and suffer the same discrimination that white workers suffer. We have, in addition to this, to espouse the cause of the white workers, only being careful that we do not in this way allow them to jeopardize our cause."[11]

Du Bois here tries to reconcile the political challenge facing the revolutionary left in his time, mainly joining together support for anti-colonial and national self-determination struggles—the problems taken up by McKay and the Comintern— with the building of broad working-class unity and proletarian internationalism. It was towards this end that the Bolshevik leader Lenin had written his 1914 essay "The Right to Self-Determination." Lenin there provided the initial analysis for what would become the Communist International's codified support for national liberation struggles, including the right of African-Americans to "secede" from the American South, as part of the building of international proletarian unity. Lenin's ideas would over time alter Du Bois's own perspective on the colonial question:

> The proletariat of Russia is faced with a twofold, or rather, a two-sided task: to combat nationalism of every kind, above all, Great-Russian nationalism; to recognize, not only fully equal rights, for all nations in general, but also equality of rights as regards polity, i.e., the right of nations to self-determination, to secession. And at the same time, it is their task, in the interests of a successful struggle against all and every kind, of nationalism among all nations to preserve the unity of the proletarian struggle and the proletarian organizations, amalgamating these organizations into a close knit international association, despite bourgeois strivings for national exclusiveness. Complete equality of rights for all nations; the right of nations to self-determination; the unity of workers of all nations—such is the national programme that Marxism, the experience of the whole world, and the experience of Russia, teach the workers.[12]

Yet in the years immediately following the Russian Revolution, Du Bois's ideas on national self-determination were still tied to the gradualist Pan-African movement agenda for African decolonization. In 1919, approximately 60 representatives met in Paris to hold the first official Pan-African Congress after the 1900 founding. Crucial to assisting Du Bois with the organizing was Blaise Diagne, a member of the French Parliament from Senegal. Also in attendance were John Hope, William Walling, and George Jackson, an African-American missionary living in the Congo. Diagne's position as French parliamentarian, and loyalty to it, and the small representation of Africans, severely limited the response of the Congress to the problem of decolonization. Rather than calling for outright independence, the Congress passed a resolution calling for direct supervision of the colonies by the new League of Nations in order to prevent their economic exploitation. It also called for the end of slavery and capital punishment for colonial subjects. In 1921, the Pan-African Congress met in London and released a "Manifesto" calling for the League of Nations to develop an "international institution for the study of Negro problems" and of an "international section in the Labor Bureau of the League of Nations, charged with the protection of native labor."[13] A third Pan-African Congress in Lisbon in 1923 was poorly organized and attended and resulted in similar resolutions. In total, the post-war Congresses represented Pan-Africanism's failure to develop an independent mass political base of opposition to imperial rule and a compromised, elitist and reformist orientation to the question of colonial self-determination.

Du Bois was gradually moved to a more radical political criticism of imperialism by a constellation of events in the 1920s. First was increasing personal anger and disappointment at the League of Nations refusal to undo colonization, and the imperialist countries' bankrupt avowals of "self-determination" which did not extend to the colonies. Second was a period of stagnation in the Pan-African Congress. For a variety of reasons, the organization lost steam after its 1922 meeting. It met only once, in 1927 in Harlem, before the momentous gathering in Manchester, England in 1945. The Harlem meeting, which drew nearly 200 delegates, mainly reiterated calls for more African autonomy, but plans for a fourth meeting in 1929 never came to fruition. Third and most important was Du Bois's closer attention to events in the Soviet Union. That attention came from multiple sources. One was the intense anti-Bolshevik propaganda in American newspapers which Du Bois understood as American nationalism and chauvinism. Another was the influence of Lala Lajpat Rai, the Hindu nationalist and anti-colonialist. Rai had arrived in the U.S. in 1907 then returned during World War I having been run out of India by the British for anti-colonial agitation. Within a short time of his arrival he befriended Du Bois, who assisted Rai in his efforts to study and understand the experience of African-Americans in the U.S., a special purpose of his visit and stay. After 1917, Rai showed growing enthusiasm for the Russian Revolution. He expressed appreciation for Bolshevik support for Indian national liberation struggle, singling out for praise the Bolsheviks' relinquishing of Ottoman territories once held by the Tsar as a "monumental step towards true world democracy," and in 1919 declaring that Soviet Russia "represents that the world is for all and not for the few who happen to be in possession at this minute."[14] Rai in turn would mentor Du Bois in elements of India's anti-colonial movement. It was during this period of Rai's influence, for example, that Du Bois would describe African-Americans as a "bound colony of the United States just as India is of England [sic]"— the most striking and immediate formulation in his thought to show the influence of Comintern policy on both colonial national self-determination and its relationship to African-Americans. The statement is direct evidence of the influence on Du Bois of discussions in Moscow joined by Claude McKay and Harry Haywood of African-Americans as an "oppressed national minority."[15]

Finally, there were on-the-ground political stirrings in the U.S. that pushed Du Bois's attention towards Communism and revolution. The Comintern directed the American Communist Party to form new organizations and recruit black workers. In 1925, Du Bois declined an invitation from African-American Communist Party member Lovett Fort-Whitman to attend the founding meeting of the American Negro Labor Congress (ANLC) in Chicago, a new Communist-front organization (one which inspired Du Bois to choose Chicago as a setting for his novel *Dark Princess*). The formation of the ANLC was a direct result of the Communist International pressuring the U.S. Communist Party to emphasize the fight against racism in the workers' movement. Du Bois supported the ANLC and the efforts of the Communists to support black labor in his public writings. The strategy helped renew Du Bois's attention to the state of the revolution: by December 1925, he was encouraging readers to "stand before the astounding effort of Soviet Russia to organize the industrial world with open mind and listening ears."[16]

It is no surprise then that Du Bois in 1926 decided to visit the Soviet Union for the first time to examine the revolution for himself. He arrived in Kronstadt in late summer, traveling from there to Moscow and then on to Nizhni Novgorod, Kiev and Odessa. By the time of his arrival, the revolution was already in crisis. Lenin's death in 1923 and what Duncan Hallas calls the "Thermidor" of industrial decline and low labor productivity were already evident. In his unpublished manuscript "Russia and America," Du Bois recounts the "stark poverty," "ragged and wild children of war and famine"[17] he saw on city streets. Politically, the revolution was also already being set back by Stalin's ascension to power: by the time Du Bois landed in Krondstadt, Trotsky along with Grigory Zinoviev, Lev Kamenev and others had already joined the "United Opposition" to Stalin; by mid-summer of that year, Stalin would strip them of their Politburo membership and party titles. By the following year, Bolshevik Party membership would drop from 430,000 to 135,000, and Stalin was compiling an enemies list and affirming the strength of the secret police to defend his power.[18]

Yet Du Bois reported on none of these developments, returning from his Soviet visit enthralled with the revolution. "If what I have seen with my eyes and heard with my ears is Bolshevism, then I am a Bolshevik," he wrote for *The Crisis*. Scholars seeking explanation for Du Bois's seemingly uncritical enthusiasm need to attend carefully to the written record of his visit and read between its lines. First, Du Bois arrived in the Soviet Union with no primary knowledge of details of the state of the revolution. He also did not speak or read Russian. He was in many ways a political tourist. He also arrived with a predilection to defend the revolution fostered by anti-Bolshevik press coverage in the U.S. Du Bois knew to be American propaganda.

Du Bois's visit was also carefully managed by his hosts to avoid confrontation with dire aspects of the revolution. Put another way, his visit was carefully managed statecraft. Thus Du Bois denies, probably accurately, ever seeing knowledge of political repression—"I know nothing of political prisoners, secret police and underground government"—though his denial affirms his general knowledge of their existence. He instead visited both the Communist University for Eastern Peoples and the Chinese University in Moscow, where he was impressed by the Russian commitment to the education of national minorities, what he called the "faces of its races—Russians, Ukrainians, Jews, Tartars, Gypsies, Caucasians, Armenians and Chinese."[19] He also saw in the theater a production of Vsevolod Meyerhold's *Hail China!*, a play commemorating the Shanghai worker uprisings that year. These preliminary vistas lead Du Bois to rhapsodize: "Russia seems to me the only modern country where people are not more or less taught and encouraged to despise and look down on some group or race. I know countries where race and color prejudice show only slight manifestations but no country where race and color prejudice seems so absolutely absent." Du Bois then adds for good measure, "anywhere in America I would get anything from curiosity to insult. In Moscow, I pass unheeded."[20]

Like Claude McKay, Langston Hughes, Paul Robeson, and other African-Americans who visited the Soviet Union after 1917, Du Bois's remarks on the absence of racism was meant as a stinging critique of U.S. racism, on one hand, and an affirmation of the Bolshevik dedication to combating "chauvinism" and racism of all forms. The endorsement is in Du Bois's case at first experiential, but deeper into his account in "Russia and America" Du Bois begins to affirm Soviet state policy. He recounts for example a visit to the State Printing Office. Du Bois observes workers there creating books in more than 100 languages. Next to it is an attached school with "A hundred apprentices—Jewish, Chinese, Tartar, Arabic" sent to work by trade unions at public expense. Du Bois then gives a concentrated description of their work:

> They are fixing and comparing letters of the alphabets by all sorts of devices. They have German, English and American equipment, but German is cheapest and English and German firms give credit terms. They spend 250,000 rubles a month on the work. They spent 500,000 rubles on equipment last year and will spend 4,000 next. They set here, print out and bind, photograph and make plates, repair and build machines. It is a little nation of nations, working happily together.[21]

Du Bois here dramatizes the "two-sided" aspiration of Soviet policy to support "the right of nations to self-determination" in order to "preserve the unity of the proletarian struggle and the proletarian organizations, amalgamating these organizations into a close knit international association." (In our next chapter, we will see how Du Bois returned to use the phrase "nation of nations" to describe his temporary program for black economic cooperatives as an alternative to capitalism, further evidence of how deeply the concept impacted his thinking.) Du Bois's adaptation, even in loose form, of this fundamentally Leninist framework was to become the most important guiding principle of Du Bois's early support for Bolshevism, and the most long-term influence on his support for world Communist revolution. It provided fuel for what David Levering Lewis called the "anticapitalist fire" Du Bois showed on his return to the U.S. from the Soviet Union in late 1926 and a conviction that the Soviets could indeed become "champions of the darker world." Thus after publishing two glowing reports of his Soviet visit in *The Crisis*, "Russia, 1926" and "I Am a Bolshevik," Du Bois plunged into work on his second novel, *Dark Princess: A Romance* (1928), an allegory of his Bolshevik baptism.

Dark Princess tells the story of Matthew Towne, a young African-American whose aspirations to become a physician are cut short by racism. Alienated from his home land, he goes into self-imposed exile in Berlin, where he meets and falls in love with Kautilya, a high caste Indian princess descended from several generations of royalty. The novel's setting marks it as Du Bois's book about efforts by the Communist International to build world revolution: Berlin was where exiled Indian revolutionaries like the Bengali nationalist Virendranath Chattopadhyaya and his American lover Agnes Smedley gathered during and after World War I to raise funds (and munitions) to overthrow British colonialism back home with the support of the Bolsheviks. The book's opening pages show Kautilya as the agent behind an internationalist contingent of aristocratic Chinese, Arabs, Japanese, and Egyptians who seek colonial independence, a loosely-veiled allusion to participants in KUTVU, or the University of the Toilers of the East in the Soviet Union (whose attendees included Sun Yat Sen and representatives from Arab Communist Parties).

The Princess has in fact recently returned from Moscow where she has been "inoculated with Bolshevism of a mild but dangerous type" including the desire to unite "Pan-Africa" with "Pan-Asia." Du Bois could not be clearer that he is speaking about the aspirations of the Bolsheviks.

The novel's plot makes the Comintern theme of the novel even more explicit: Matthew and the Princess separate temporarily, Matthew heading back to the U.S. where he becomes involved in an act of revolutionary terrorism planned by a Marcus Garvey-like nationalist named Perigua. The plan is foiled by the Princess's intervention. The two of them then undergo a joint proletarianization essential to their attempt to build working-class unity from erstwhile national liberation struggles at home and back in India: Matthew as a train porter and the Princess as a domestic worker and box factory employee. Du Bois chooses these symbolic locations which in the time of the novel were central points of Communist and socialist labor agitation and unionization efforts (A. Philip Randolph for example forming the Brotherhood of Sleeping Car Porters, the first national black union in the United States). As they labor, Matthew and the Princess declaim their internationalism in the loosely-veiled language of Comintern policy. At their reunion at Matthew's maternal home, the former slave state of Virginia, where his ancestors toiled and his slave-descended mother still lives, Kautilya speaks of Matthew's life as African-American:

> You are not free in Chicago, nor New York. But here in Virginia you are at the end of a black world. The black belt of the Congo, Haiti, and Jamaica, like a red arrow, up into the heart of white America. Thus I see a mighty synthesis: you can work in Africa and Asia right here in America if you work in the Black Belt . . .
>
> I have seen slaves ruling in Chicago and they did not do nearly as bad as princes in Russia . . . How truly you have put it! Workers unite, men cry, while in truth always thinkers who do not work have tried to unite workers who do not think. Only working thinkers can unite thinking workers.[22]

Du Bois here paraphrases the Soviet Comintern line of self-determination for the southern "Black Belt" approved at the Third Comintern in the same year as the publication of *Dark Princess*. The novel ends with the announcement that Matthew and Kautilya will bear a child, deemed "Messenger and Messiah to all the Darker Worlds!"[23] As Alyn Weinbaum has noted, Du Bois here conjures up a politics of mixed-race biological reproduction to counter both white supremacist eugenics discourse about the need to exterminate "lesser" non-white races, and to mark the "rising tide" of anti-colonial political currents sweeping the Pan-Asian and Pan-African worlds during the 1920s. The novel offers an allegory of world revolution and global decolonization hatched in a "global south" linking Matthew's home in the Black Belt to the Princess's "Bwodpur." The novel shows for the first time Du Bois's fascination with, and dedication to, India's decolonization as a companion to black liberation struggle in the U.S.—a theme to which we shall return. It was for this reason in part that Du Bois later referred to the novel as his "favorite" among his creative works.

Mark Van Wienan has argued that *Dark Princess* shows Du Bois moving from "Second" to "Third" International politics, from gradualist reformer to Leninist revolutionary.[24] As we will see in the next chapter, that judgment is true within limits. But the Soviet Revolution of 1917, the formation of the Comintern, the struggles of the Pan-African movement, and the radicalization of many African-Americans and Afro-Caribbeans in the aftermath of the Russian revolution did shift the direction of Du Bois's thinking in significant ways we have documented here. Du Bois became a more *forward-thinking* revolutionary in the 1920s, more optimistic about the possibilities of black people, Asians, and workers of the world to make a world-historical change. His novel *Dark Princess* even includes the prophetic line "The Dark World goes free in 1952"—a prediction of end of colonialism that did not miss the mark by all that much.

At the same time, Du Bois's failure to document any of the setbacks of the Russian Revolution during his 1926 visit, especially the political repression settling in under Stalin, anticipated a refusal or denial in years to come of those same phenomena. Du Bois's enthusiasm about the 1926 Revolution was the enthusiasm of a latecomer to the Revolution and of someone not as yet trained in revolutionary theory and practice. Coming from America, the heart of capitalist empire with which he was growing increasingly disenchanted, Du Bois exaggerated differences and Soviet "glories" to make that disenchantment clear. The most important lesson of the decade of his first Russian visit was mainly that he had to learn more, and know more, about Marxism and socialism. The Great Depression just around the corner only deepened that sense of urgency.

5

The Depression,
Black Reconstruction,
and Du Bois's Asia Turn

Du Bois returned from the Soviet Union in 1928 with new ideas and new hopes about alternatives to capitalism. "If Russia fails," he wrote, "reason in industry fails. If Russia succeeds, gradually every modern state will socialize industry and the greater the Russian success, the less revolution."[1] Du Bois began to imagine new modernization programs that might pull the train of African-American (and global) labor forward. From 1928 through the end of the 1930s and the Great Depression, Du Bois entered into an economistic phase of his thought which attempted to programmatize this conception.

This stage of his life began as a course of self-training in Marx's writings and was shaped by events in the global depression, especially the emergence of economic cooperatives in different parts of the world. At the same time, Du Bois began an immersive study of American capitalism's own history, centering on the Civil War and the institution of slavery. The result of that study, his 1935 book *Black Reconstruction*, is the pivot point of his intellectual and political development. As we shall see, *Black Reconstruction* was Du Bois's own "manifesto" of American capitalism and the role of black workers in it. The book argues for African-American self-emancipation during the Civil War and after as what Du Bois called an "experiment of Marxism." The book is also Du Bois's first, full-fledged effort to develop a theory about the relationship of U.S. capitalism and slavery to world imperialism, and the prospects for black working-class struggle to lead a challenge to both. Finally, the book is monumental

W.E.B. Du Bois, Nina Du Bois, and James Weldon Johnson in Great Barrington, c. 1930. W.E.B. Du Bois Papers (MS 312). Special Collections and University Archives, University of Massachusetts Amherst Libraries

for exposing the racist historiography of slavery and the Civil War that dominated scholarship up until Du Bois's writing of the book.

In many ways, the period of the 1930s shows Du Bois advancing himself, along with contemporary Marxists and leaders of world revolutionary struggle, onto a new global stage as a vanguard activist and scholar: his use of Marxist analysis in *Black Reconstruction*, and his attempt to understand slavery's role in the development of global capitalism, culminated in a second trip abroad in 1936, this one a return to the Soviet Union, but included first-time visits to Japan and China, epicenters of what Du Bois perceived as a nascent world revolutionary situation. By the time of his return from that trip, Du Bois was more committed than ever to support for world revolution against capitalism and the decolonization of the planet.

On February 15, 1929, Du Bois wrote a letter to Algernon Lee, chairman of the New York State Socialist Party, urging him to address the problem of racism in the U.S. labor movement. Du Bois felt doing so would help attract black workers to socialism. "If the Negro does not embrace the doctrines of socialism" he wrote, "his advance will increase difficulties of the labor movement."[2] The letter came on the heels of a failed attempt by Du Bois to form an Interracial Labor Commission of the American Federation of Labor, the NAACP and the Brotherhood of Sleeping Car Porters. The latter was the first all-black union in the U.S. headed by A. Philip Randolph, Jr. Du Bois's intensified interest in labor unity reflected a newfound Bolshevik spirit imbibed in the Soviet Union refracted through events around him in the U.S.: in 1931, for example, the Communist Party would organize more than 800 black farmers into a new union and form the League of Struggle for Negro Rights in the South.[3]

Also in 1931, nine young black men riding a train across Alabama in search of work were accused of raping two white women on the train when they disembarked near Scottsboro. One of the women shortly recanted the allegations, but the charges stuck, and a prolonged trial began resulting in numerous convictions. Both the NAACP, Du Bois's affiliate organization, and the International Labor Defense, the legal arm of the Communist Party, rushed to defend the "Scottsboro Boys" as they were named by the popular and left-wing press. The CP argued that the boys were members of the black proletariat railroaded both by racism and capitalism. The NAACP generally ignored the class dimension of the accusations, holding the boys up as race martyrs and a reminder of the many black men in the U.S. lynched for alleged sexual interest in white women. In his public writings on the case, Du Bois protested that the Communist Party was using the trial "to foment revolution in the United States," a position he felt would make African-Americans "shock troops" in a deeply racist south.[4] This moment should be read dialectically with Du Bois's essay published the same year, "The Negro and Marxism" in which Du Bois asserted that racism remained so deep in the U.S. that it would forestall a successful workers' revolution. As Du Bois put it, "even when the lines of class struggle are closely defined and the Russian experience is so definite that it does not disprove but rather strengthens my belief."[5]

And yet, still enthralled by his visit to the Soviet Union, Du Bois dedicated much of his time during the years 1931–34 to a self-directed study of Marxism. He read *Capital*, the *Communist Manifesto*, and most likely *The German Ideology* and the *Eighteenth Brumaire of Louis Bonaparte*. These materials informed a series of lectures Du Bois began in 1932 at Atlanta University on "Imperialism in the Sudan, 1400 to 1700" and "The Economic Future of Black America," as well as new courses on the topics "Karl Marx and the Negro" and "Economic History of the Negro." In 1933, he indicated a desire to publish a series of articles in *The Crisis* intended to be a "rapprochement between black America and socialism" with topics like "The 'Class Struggle of the Black Proletariat and Bourgeosie,' Punishment, Charity and the Black Proletariat," and "The Dictatorship of the Black Proletariat."[6] Simultaneous with this ambition, Du Bois was hard at work reading all available sources on slavery and the Civil War in the process of writing *Black Reconstruction*.

These multiple plans of study all came together in that finished book. In the interval came an important, if misguided, first step effort by Du Bois to create "rapprochement between black America and socialism." Du Bois noted that in 1919 the Bolsheviks consolidated under state control economic cooperatives as part of a "transitional" program to socialism. In *The Crisis*, Du Bois began publishing a series of articles advocating for black "producers' cooperation" of goods and "increased economic independence." The cooperative, black capitalism by another name, was intended, as Mark Van Wienan notes, to be a "strategy of self-directed social democracy for black America, and by extension for people of color throughout the world."[7] As Du Bois put it:

> Present organization of industry for private profit and control of government is doomed to disaster. It must change and fall if civilization survives. The foundation of its present world-wide power is the slavery and semi-slavery of the colored world including the American Negroes. Until the colored man, yellow, red, brown, and black, becomes free, articulate, intelligent and the receiver of a decent income, white capital will use the profit derived from his degradation to keep white labor in chains.[8]

Du Bois's cooperative program was meant as a non-violent strategy of self-determination to bring about a social and economic revolution in the conditions of African-Americans. As he wrote in 1934:

> With the use of their political power as consumers, and their brainpower . . . Negroes can develop in the United States an economic nation within a nation, able to work through inner cooperation, to found its own institutions, to educate its genius, and at the same time without mob violence or extremes of race hatred, to keep in helpful touch and cooperate with the mass of the nation. *This has happened more often than most people realize, in the case of groups not so obviously separated from the mass of people as are American Negroes.* It must happen in our case, or there is no hope for the Negro in America.[9]

This excerpt and the title of the essay from which it comes, "A Negro Nation Within the Nation," clearly shows Du Bois attempting to apply in idiosyncratic fashion self-determination principles to African-American life in the U.S. The title, for example, recalls the phrase Du Bois used to describe workers at the Soviet print shop—"a little nation of nations" as a sign of general approval of the Soviet policy on self-determination for its ethnic minorities. Yet strikingly absent from his formulation of black cooperative economics, as journalist and labor organizer George Streator pointed out to Du Bois in a sharp exchange of letters, was the role of labor, of labor exploitation, of class struggle. How, Streator asked Du Bois, would black workers possibly "separate" themselves from capitalism as long as capitalism existed?

Du Bois's continued study of the class formation of the U.S. and readings in Marxism would lead to a shift in his thought meant to address the question of labor. In June 1936, Du Bois published what he called his "creed for American Negroes" in the *Pittsburgh Courier,* one of the country's preeminent African-American newspapers to which he was a contributor. The essay enumerated, manifesto-style, an eleven-point argument about the centrality of the black working class to history. It urged black workers to join the labor movement, and argued, "We believe that Workers' Councils organized by Negroes for interracial understanding should strive to fight race prejudice in the working class." It continued: "We believe in the ultimate triumph of some form of Socialism the world over; that is, common ownership and control of the means of production and equality of income."[10] Du Bois also invoked workers' councils—or Soviets—central to the Bolshevik revolution of 1917, of Chinese industrial strikes of 1926 and 1927, and of Spanish workers uprisings—as examples for black workers to follow. In total, the evolution of Du Bois's thought from consumerist cooperatives to workers councils shows Du Bois formulating what he called in a letter to Streator "a realistic approach to a democratic state in which the exploitation of labor is stopped, and the political power is in the hands of the workers."[11]

But it was in his magisterial book of 1935, *Black Reconstruction*, that Du Bois first found historical example and justification for this political ambition. Reconstruction is the name given by U.S. historians to the period from 1865–77 in U.S. history when the federal government attempted to administer the former confederate states' transition out of war and defeat. Under federal military supervision and decree, southern states emancipated their slaves, dismantled much of the plantation cotton system, and were compelled by the newly-passed thirteenth and fourteenth amendments to, in theory, deliver citizenship, including the vote, to African-Americans. The federal reconstruction program also included a Freedmen's Bureau and Freedmen's Schools meant to distribute resources and educational opportunity for the first time to newly freed blacks. Reconstruction saw the black vote deliver to southern offices the first-ever elected black officials in the region, small-scale gains in black property and land ownership, and a temporary decline in formal, and previously legal, forms of racism directed against African-Americans in the south.

Du Bois developed an entirely new and revolutionary theory to explain this period in American history. Typical paternal and racist Civil War historiography of his time emphasized the benevolence of white figures like Abraham Lincoln, and used racist stereotype to denigrate African-Americans as incapable of achieving their own freedom. Du Bois instead interpreted the end of slavery, the Civil War, and the Reconstruction period as the first time in U.S. history that the black working class undertook its own wide-scale self-emancipation. Du Bois pointed out that 200,000 African-Americans had fled the plantation during the Civil War, what he called a "general strike" against slavery. Many of them joined the Union Army, and helped turn the victorious battle against the South. After emancipation and during Reconstruction, African-Americans organized amongst themselves to redistribute land, resources, education and social benefits. It was this process which Du Bois referred to, idiosyncratically, as an "experiment of Marxism": "As the Negro laborers organized separately, there came slowly to realization the fact that here was not only separate organization but a separation in leading ideas, because among Negroes, and particularly in the South, there was being put into force one of the most extraordinary experiments of Marxism that the world, before the Russian revolution, had seen."[12]

What did Du Bois mean by calling black worker self-activity an "experiment of Marxism"? As Cedric Robinson notes, the Russian Revolution was a "framework" for Du Bois's interpretation of the U.S. Civil War. Du Bois, he rightly argues, perceived the rebellion of black and white slaves and southern peasants (100,000 whites, Robinson notes, also fled the plantations during the war) as a reminder that the Russian Revolution had broken out in a largely backward, agrarian state. Du Bois in effect argued that slaves were acting prefiguratively as what Harry Haywood called "Black Bolsheviks" in the name of their own freedom. More germane still to his idea of a Marxist "experiment," Du Bois's analysis of the Civil War had been influenced by a book titled *Lincoln, Labor and Slavery: A Chapter from the Social History of America*, first published in 1913 by the German-born socialist Herman Schluter. Schluter's book pointed out that many northern U.S. workers were anti-slavery, aligning themselves with Karl Marx and the International Workingmen's Association in London which during the Civil War appealed to Lincoln to end the war and free the slaves. The Civil War gave Marx his most famous declaration on interracial proletarian unity: "White skin labor can not be free wherein the black skin it is branded."[13]

Du Bois cited Schluter, and Marx's letters to Lincoln, in *Black Reconstruction*, in trying to develop a Marxist perspective on the Civil War and Reconstruction as a class struggle. On one side, Du Bois wrote, were slaves, former slaves, poor whites and white workers; on the other northern industrialists and southern plantation owners. Ultimately, Du Bois wrote, Reconstruction ended when the latter conspired with southern elites to extend the domain of capitalism into the South in order to preserve ruling class wealth. This was for Du Bois a great tragedy. The formal end of Reconstruction meant that while black slaves were now free, an *interracial working class* that had worked to free itself was defeated. Yet even the short-term victory was in Du Bois's analysis an important workers' revolution. As Du Bois put it: "The unending tragedy of Reconstruction is the utter inability of the American mind to grasp its real significance . . . We are still too blind and infatuated to conceive of the emancipation of the laboring class in half the nation as a revolution comparable to the upheavals in France in the past, and in Russia, Spain, India and China today."[14]

Du Bois's comparison of Reconstruction to completed or ongoing attempted revolutions elsewhere in the world also demonstrated a new Marxist internationalism in his thought. Du Bois argued that the collapse of Reconstruction was significant for opening wide the gates for capitalist development, and U.S. imperialism. Du Bois also argued that the black worker under slavery in the nineteenth century was what Marx called a "pivot" in the development of world capitalism generally. He was representative, as Du Bois put it, of "That dark and vast sea of human labor in China and India, the South Seas and all Africa . . . that great majority of mankind, on whose bent and broken backs rest today the founding stones of modern industry,"[15] another version of Marx's "primitive accumulation" thesis. Finally, Du Bois's thundering conclusion sealed his dialectical analysis: "Out of the exploitation of the dark proletariat comes the Surplus Value filched from human beasts which, in cultured lands, the Machine and harnessed Power veil and conceal. The emancipation of labor is the freeing of that basic majority of workers who are yellow, brown and black."[16]

From his initial premise of black self-emancipation to this conclusion of the Civil War and Reconstruction as turning points in the history of Western capitalism Du Bois's *Black Reconstruction* deserves a place alongside C.L.R. James's *Black Jacobins,* on the Haitian Revolution, and Marx's *The Civil War in France*, on the Paris Commune, as watershed works in the Marxist tradition on the meaning of revolutions led by workers from below. Indeed, James's book on the Haitian Revolution, published in 1936, was deeply influenced by Du Bois's work on slavery and reconstruction. Du Bois's analysis of slaves as agents of their own emancipation helped to develop James's analysis of Haitian slaves as "Jacobin" revolutionaries. James gave direct credit for Du Bois's influence in his 1938 book *A History of Pan-African Revolt*. It is also quite probable that Du Bois's appropriation of the term "dictatorship of the proletariat" to describe black self-governance in *Black Reconstruction* came from Marx's use of that term to describe the communards takeover of Paris in 1871. Du Bois, in other words, understood black Reconstruction, as Marx did the Commune, as an "experiment of Marxism."

Du Bois here also reveals insight, contradiction and shortcomings in his attempt to develop a Marxist methodology. Like Marx, Du Bois perceived the Civil War as a potential war for the emancipation of the working class that did not succeed. Du Bois's interpretation of the black working class (and portions of the white working class) as seeking its own self-emancipation demonstrated a commitment to socialism from below. The characterization of fugitive slaves fleeing the plantation as a "general strike" was an idiosyncratic—but not entirely wrong—application of Marx's analysis of labor self-activity.

At the same time, the federal government of the North was never an emancipatory force for the working class. The victory of capital in the Civil War assured that the Civil War would bring about a "bourgeois revolution" that would advance and extend capitalism and capitalist interests. At best, Du Bois's use of the phrase "experiment of Marxism" to describe black worker self-activity during and after the Civil War should be understood as a general euphemism for something like black self-determination as articulated by the Comintern in its Black Belt thesis. But this analogy too breaks down on inspection: chained or emancipated slaves did not live under colonial rule.

These judgments, and misjudgments, give us insight into several aspects of Du Bois's broader thought about revolutions and revolutionary capacities. First, from the time he joined the Pan-African movement in 1900, the African-American working class was for Du

Bois a potential vanguard in both Pan-African liberation struggle and class struggle. Second, Du Bois's argument in *Black Reconstruction* that white workers were given a "wage of whiteness"—social benefits and political access—in exchange for their allegiance to the white ruling class demonstrated his understanding of Marx's own insistence that black and white labor could only rise together.[17] Third, the final chapter of *Black Reconstruction*, "The Propaganda of History," which attacked racist historiography of the Civil War and slavery, announced Du Bois's break with bourgeois historiography and method as part of his transition to becoming a Marxist scholar and activist. Fourth, Du Bois's assertion that the end of Reconstruction helped to usher into an age of rampant capitalist expansion and imperialism has been amply borne out by historians who have come after him. Finally, *Black Reconstruction*'s role as a "pivot" in his own turn to Marxist methodology, and eventually, Communism, has ironic prescience. By the time of the book's publication, 1935, Du Bois's peers on the black left, including A. Phillip Randolph, Claude McKay, C.L.R. James, and George Padmore, all one-time enthusiasts for the Bolshevik Revolution, had begun or completed their break with the Soviet Union over Stalin's hijacking of the Revolution. Du Bois was then moving, as he did much of the rest of his life, against the grain even of some of his closest colleagues and intellectual peers by constellating uncritical admiration for the Russian Revolution. This, however, should not obscure the overall achievement of Du Bois's book, which stands to this day as his most important, and most radical, contribution to U.S. and African-American history.

In his novel *Dark Princess*, Du Bois included representatives of anti-colonial movements in China and Japan as symbols of their place in his Comintern-influenced scheme of world revolution. Du Bois had supported Japan as a "champion of the darker world" since its 1905 victory over Russia. He cheered on its efforts in the 1920s to build a capitalist state that could compete with "white" Western Europe especially. Throughout the 1920s and early years of the Depression, Du Bois also perceived China as a colored challenger to Western imperialist states. He wrote favorably of China's 1911 Republican Revolution and included China's anti-colonial struggle in

Black Reconstruction as an important battle of the world's non-white working class.

The emergence of Japanese imperialism after World War I was initially accommodated to Du Bois's worldview by the logic that it was better for a non-white state to colonize than a white one. Thus Du Bois initially excused Japanese expansion into Ethiopia and China as stepping stones necessary for its development into a global power than could compete with the imperial West. This same worldview caused Du Bois for a time to denigrate China as a comparative Asian doormat —the Uncle Tom of the East—which should take a cue from Japan's example and become itself a world leader.

The blatant and uninformed naiveté of these assessments are primarily attributable to Du Bois's lack of understanding of Japanese and Chinese history and to his still evolving understanding of Marxism and capitalism. Later in life, Du Bois admitted that his early appraisals of both Japan and China were owing to ignorance on both counts. But it was also his "Marxist turn" of the 1930s that drew Du Bois to closer study and engagement with both China and Japan. In 1936, immediately after publishing *Black Reconstruction*, Du Bois decided to visit the Soviet Union a second time, but this time to make separate visits to both China and Japan. In each instance, Du Bois wrote, it was "socialism" or the prospect of socialism that drew him. In the case of Japan, Du Bois perceived the philosophy of Japanese Social Gospelist Toyohiko Kagawa as an inspiration for his own confidence in cooperative economics as a bridge to socialism. In China's case, while he was not yet advocating a Communist victory over the Nationalist movement, he wished the country to throw out Western influence minimally as a step to ending its conflict with Japan. Indeed in 1933, Du Bois had written apoplectically that China and Japan must cease conflict that only preyed into Western hands: "The real rulers of the world today . . . are blood-sucking imperial tyrants who see only one thing in the quarrel of China and Japan, and that is a chance to crush and exploit both. Unmask them, Asia. Tear apart their double faces and double tongues and unite in peace."[18]

Yet the weakness of Du Bois's understanding of both Japanese imperialism and Chinese historical oppression lay primarily in a faulty understanding of both capitalism and Marxism. In late 1936, upon arriving in Japan, Du Bois wrote, "The accomplishment of Japan has been to realize the meaning of European aggression on the darker peoples, to discover the secret of the white man's power, and then without revolutionary violence to change her whole civilization and attitude toward the world, so as to emerge in the twentieth century the equal in education, technique, health, industry and art of any nation on earth."[19] But because the "Europe which she copied" is no "perfect land," "Japan is called again to lead world revolution, and lead it with the minimum of violence and upheaval. In the nineteenth century, Japan saved the world from slavery to Europe. In the twentieth century she is called to save the world from slavery to capital."[20]

The strangeness of Du Bois's analysis is brought home on his report of a visit to Japanese-occupied Manchuria, where Du Bois praises the state-controlled and state-managed Southern Manchuria Railroad Company. The SMRC was central to Japan's development of the East Asian Cooperative Body, described by Onishi as "the idea that a collectivized Asian economy provided a step towards a more 'just' social order."[21] Du Bois fails to register the brutal oppression of labor in Manchuria, the fact that the SMRC sits on Occupied Chinese land, and that profit extraction is feeding Japan's own imperialist war against the Chinese.

Du Bois's racialist nationalism in favor of Japan, motivated by anti-Eurocentrism, bleaches capitalism of its universal particulars like surplus value and allows it to pass as benign modernization. Yet within a year, Du Bois had reversed his analysis of Japan's empire, and expelled it for all intents and purposes from his framework of Asian liberation. Two events were central to this shift in perspective. Japan's invasion of Nanjing in 1937, its massacre of thousands of innocents, unmasked naked Japanese imperialism and disabused Du Bois of further support. More central to Du Bois's understanding of capitalism was a visit to Shanghai in early winter, 1937, immediately on the heels of his trip to Japan and Manchuria. In Shanghai, Du Bois comments on both China's central place in the history of Western imperialism—"Three things attract white Europe to China: cheap women, cheap child-labor; cheap men," he writes[22] and on something absent from his account of both Tokyo and Manchuria, namely labor exploitation:

> Always there is this mass of labor. Labor that has never learned to revolt, to demand, and is only beginning to strike in a few mass industries—ideal labor for profits. The wage is low, and only balanced by still lower cost of living. The rickshaw man drags you, running five miles or more in a half hour for a cent and a half or three cents. A gardener gets five dollars a month with room and board, that is rice and a bit else; a factory hand, I have been told, may get 12 cents a day.[23]

This moment of recognition functioned like something of an epiphany for Du Bois. In later writings, including his *Autobiography* and his fictional Mansart Trilogy, Du Bois re-narrated his Shanghai visit of 1937 in order to underscore his failure to perceive accurately China's place in the long history of both feudalism and capitalism. In his *Autobiography*, written just before his death but published posthumously, Du Bois would write:

> I used to weep for American Negroes, as I saw what indignities and repressions and cruelties they had passed; but as I read Chinese history in these last months and had it explained to me stripped of Anglo-Saxon lies, I know that no depths of Negro slavery in America have plumbed such abysses as the Chinese have seen for 2,000 years and more. They have seen starvation and murder; rape and prostitution; sale and slavery of children; and religion cloaked in opium and gin . . . This oppression and contempt came not only from Tartars, Mongolians, British, French, Germans and Americans, but from the Chinese themselves: Mandarins and warlords, capitalists and murdering thieves like Chiang Kai-shek; Kuomintang Socialists and intellectuals, educated abroad.[24]

By the time he returned from his visits to Japan and China in 1937, Du Bois was sobered about the meaning of "socialism" and its prospects in Asia, while still clinging stubbornly to a racialized interpretation of Asian history that persisted until very late in life:

To me the tragedy of this epoch was that Japan learned Western ways too soon and too well, and turned from Asia to Europe. She had a fine culture, an exquisite art, and an industrial technique miraculous in workmanship and adaptability. The Japanese clan was an effective social organ and her art expression was unsurpassed. She might have led Asia and the world into a new era. But her headstrong leaders chose to apply Western imperialism to her domination of the east, and Western profit-making replaced eastern idealism. If she had succeeded, it might have happened that she would have spread her culture and achieved a co-prosperity sphere with freedom of soul. Perhaps![25]

Du Bois's interpretation of Japanese expansion and domination as an application of "Western imperialism" over "eastern idealism" belies his own idealized (and mildly Orientalist) interpretation of history. It was of a piece with his earlier Japanese exceptionalism that forestalled criticism of its collaboration with Western capitalist powers. It also explains, as we shall see later, his excessive enthusiasm for Maoist China once 1949 revolution came into his purview. Throughout his life and career, including in his assessment of India, Du Bois often practiced a form of Third World nationalist boosterism that competed with his efforts to develop an historical materialist analysis of history. This tendency made him more vulnerable to Stalinism, dulling his capacity to understand why state capitalism was not Marxism, and exuding a form of nationalist enthusiasm for "Socialism in One Country."

Assessing the near decade of Du Bois's life from 1929 to the end of the 1930s, one sees several significant developments and changes that anticipate directions in his thought and work. Despite his bracing recognition of Japanese imperialism, Du Bois ended the decade of the 1930s more committed than ever to support for the Soviet Union. His 1936 visit to the country was brief and uneventful save to shore up enthusiasm for ongoing Stalinist projects like the forced collectivization of the kulaks. While in his 1950 manuscript "Russia and America" he lamented the loss of life and violence of collectivization, Du Bois justified the state's actions as a defense against counter-revolutionary forces. Though he was in Russia the same year as the beginnings of the purges, Du Bois also remained silent on them. Later, in his 1950 manuscript, he would similarly defend Stalin's persecution of Trotsky especially, succumbing to Stalinist propaganda that the latter was an agent of the Nazis.

These errors in political judgment should also be seen in dialectical relationship to other events of the 1930s discussed here. The global depression persuaded Du Bois that capitalism was in near total collapse, and that some alternative (be it cooperative economics, an Asian "Co-Prosperity" sphere, benevolent Japanese imperialism, or Chinese revolution) was necessary. The continuing colonization of Africa in the 1930s also deepened Du Bois's animus towards colonial-capitalism, an animus that would gather strength during World War II and culminate in the 1945 Pan-African Congress in Manchester. Likewise, the Italian invasion of Ethiopia in 1935, an event which galvanized black American defense of Ethiopia as an African motherland, and began the process of building black support for Western anti-fascism, reminded Du Bois that Africa remained central to the "roots" of global inter-imperial conflict. However, Du Bois failed to criticize the Soviet Union for supplying materials to Italy during this period, in stark contrast to his friend George Padmore, whose criticism of the Soviets was part of his own break with the Communist International.

Regarding India, Du Bois after 1929 devoted more and more public support and attention to the leadership of Gandhi. Gandhi's *swadeshi* principles of non-cooperation were in fact one stated source of Du Bois's own program of consumer production and cooperation discussed earlier. When the depression began, Du Bois invited Gandhi to provide a statement of friendship and support for African-Americans in the U.S. for *The Crisis* (he obliged). Du Bois likewise interpreted the ongoing anti-colonial movement in India as a necessary wedge against British imperialism in Africa and elsewhere, and championed Nehru's rise to power and the Indian National Congress as harbingers of the non-white world's eventual self-emancipation.

In total, the decade of the depression impressed upon Du Bois forever a desire to end capitalism for good. In 1940, Du Bois published the book *Dusk of Dawn*, which included a recasting of the

"Basic American Negro Creed" cited above, wherein Du Bois for the first time evoked the necessity of a workers' takeover of society: "We believe in the ultimate triumph of some form of Socialism the world over; that is, common ownership and control of the means of production and equality of income."[26] So fixed was the principle in Du Bois's thought that he repeated it again, word for word, in an interlude of the *Autobiography* written at the end of his life and published posthumously. The interlude was titled, simply, "Communism."

Yet for Du Bois, as always, the question of what Communism was, what it might be, and how to achieve it, remained what he called elsewhere, in a different context, the "riddle of the Sphinx." It was a riddle ever-darkened and deepened by the specter of Stalinism, which continued to distort and destroy principles of Leninism and Bolshevism even as the Soviet Union remained for many, Du Bois included, the beacon of socialist hope. It was a riddle also made complicated by Du Bois's parallel commitments to anti-colonialism, especially Pan-Africanism. It is into the breach of these contradictions that Du Bois continued to move as we enter the period of the 1940s and World War II.

6

Pan-Africanism
or Communism?

Du Bois's 1915 book *The Negro* was a study of the history of Africa and its place in world development. "There are those . . . who would write universal history and leave out Africa," Du Bois wrote in the book, angry at scholars of "western civilization" who omitted Africa from its rightful place.[1] Du Bois revised the book in 1946 into the book *The World and Africa*. The tradition now known as "Afrocentric" or African-centered scholarship on Africa includes Du Bois's work.

Du Bois visited the African continent for the first time in 1924. "And now as a sort of ambassador of Pan Africa I turn my face toward Africa," he wrote in the *The Crisis*[2] He was moved and astonished on seeing Cape Mount for the first time, "So my great great grandfather saw it two centuries ago."[3] Du Bois visited Liberia, the African country to which African-Americans had sought to repatriate in the nineteenth century in order to recover an African "homeland" stripped away by slavery.

Du Bois came to Liberia with instructions and recommendations for the Liberian President about how to develop an independent Liberian economy. He hoped to challenge colonial domination of the African economies on his visit. He told President Hughes the country should develop a 20-year plan, establish a large bank under black control, and raise capital with investment from African-Americans. Du Bois also tried to gain influence with Harvey Firestone, President of Firestone, the rubber company, which hoped to build a concession in Liberia to manufacture rubber.[4]

Du Bois traveled and spoke next to the National Congress of British West Africa in Sierra Leone, a group founded by the Ghanaian journalist and Pan-Africanist Casely Hayford. His message was one of "common action" among African people of the diaspora.[5] In all of these activities Du Bois thought African economic development was critical to its advance even if it required Western capital. Later in life he would advise African countries against Western aid, seeing it as a continuation of colonial influence.

Du Bois was emotionally smitten by Africa on this visit and described it in romantic terms. "The spell of Africa is upon me. The ancient witchery of her medicine is burning my drowsy, dreamy blood. This is not a country, it is a world,"[6] he wrote. The African trip motivated Du Bois to try and revive the Pan-African movement. In 1927, Du Bois organized the Fourth Pan-African Congress in New York City. Two hundred and eight delegates from eleven countries attended—although only three, Liberia, Sierra Leone and the Gold Coast, from Africa. Little was achieved at the meeting except for more symbolic pronouncements on the need for African unity against colonialism.

In the same year as the Congress meeting, a young Trinidadian named George Padmore (born Malcolm Nurse) joined the Communist Party of the United States, also in New York. Padmore had come to New York to attend law school. He immediately became editor of the party newspaper in Harlem, the *Negro Champion*. Padmore joined the party in the same year as the Communist International created the League Against Imperialism, its first attempt to unify anti-imperialists across the world. Padmore was attracted to Communism by the Comintern's strong declaration of support for anti-colonial self-determination. In 1929, Padmore attended the League's second congress in Frankfurt, Germany, along with prominent, emerging world dignitaries like Jawarhalal Nehru.

Eventually, Padmore would become a close friend, mentor, and political foil to W.E.B. Du Bois. Their personal relationship is symbolic of the larger relationship between Communism and Pan-Africanism in the twentieth century. At its heart was the question of whether a Stalinized Russia or decolonizing African states themselves were better suited to carry forward Africa's independence. Indeed, Padmore had been won to Communism by the Bolshevik and Comintern program for anti-colonial struggle and proletarian unity. The 1928 Third Comintern which codified the "Black Belt" thesis on African-Americans discussed earlier was also central to this question. Padmore initially supported it, Du Bois initially opposed it, but by 1935, the two were working in distant collaboration on new ideas and arguments for how the Pan-African movement, and the colonized countries generally, should create their own independence struggles. The period of World War II then should be viewed as a key turning point in the life of Du Bois and his relationship to both Pan-Africanism and international Communism. By 1945, at the famous Fifth Pan-African Congress, a new generation of African leaders, initially trained by the Communist International, declared their independence from Soviet Communism while announcing a new phase of anti-colonial internationalism. At the same time, the war deepened Du Bois's support for the Soviet Union, which was under military attack by Hitler's Germany and, soon, Cold War attack by the American state. This contradictory movement is the story of this chapter.

In 1928 George Padmore attended the Fourth Congress of the Profintern, or Red International of Labour Unions (RILU). The Profintern was the Comintern vehicle to show the autonomy of communist trade unions from "reformist" unions. The Profintern plan also included increased attention to recruiting Black workers. On July 7–9, 1930, the First International Conference of Negro Workers sponsored by the Comintern was held in Hamburg, Germany. In 1931, RILU passed a "Special Resolution on Negro Works among Negroes in the U.S. and the Colonies"—another indication of the Comintern's new perspective on African-American workers as an oppressed national minority.

Twice in this period, Padmore attacked W.E.B. Du Bois. In 1931, he published *The Life and Struggles of Negro Toilers*, accusing Du Bois and other African-Americans like Oscar DePriest of being "American Negro petty-bourgeois reformists."[7] Shortly thereafter, Padmore generated a pamphlet titled "Negro Workers and the Imperialist War—Intervention in the Soviet Union," attacking Du Bois for his "reflexive anticommunism."[8] Du Bois earned Padmore's wrath for his constant criticism of the failures of the American left, including the Communist Party, to sufficiently address racism in the working class. From Padmore's perspective, Du Bois was ignoring the special attention paid by the Communist International to Black freedom struggle after 1917, including its pressuring of the U.S. Communist Party to create the American Negro Labor Congress.

Yet by 1934, Padmore himself had broken with the Comintern, and was appealing to Du Bois to help him raise $5 million to bail out the rulers of Liberia. What had happened? Padmore's biographer says he was expelled by the Comintern's International Control Commission for working with a bourgeois formation in Liberia. Padmore said he quit because the Comintern liquidated its Negro Trade Union Committee and ceased publication of the *Negro Worker*, and because the Comintern failed to adequately support African countries like Liberia and Ethiopia seeking independence from colonial rule. Whatever the reason, Padmore's break prompted him to write to Du Bois seeking to support a Negro World Unity Congress—an effort to revitalize the Pan-African movement. It also led him over time to write one of the best-known books of the anti-colonial era, *Pan-Africanism or Communism?: The Coming Struggle for Africa*, first published in 1956, and from whence this chapter draws its title.

Yet Padmore's book presented a dichotomy—Pan-Africanism or Communism—where there was much theoretical and practical overlap, unity and dialectical synthesis. For example, after his break with the Comintern, Padmore returned to London where he began a long collaboration with fellow Trinidadian and Marxist C.L.R. James. In London, James had joined the Communist League, the first British Trotskyist organization. He was at work on two books reflecting his own turn to Trotskyism and the question of black liberation. The first, *World Revolution 1917–1936: The Rise and Fall of the Communist International*, was a scathing indictment of Stalin's reign and the Comintern for failing to support workers' struggles and anti-colonial movements in Europe, Asia and Africa. James argued that Stalin's commitment to "Socialism in One Country" was an abandonment of Leninist principles and of Trotsky's theory of "permanent revolution" which insisted on the spread of revolutions globally for any one revolution to survive.

James was also nearing completion of his historical masterpiece *The Black Jacobins*, which should also be understood as a product of his rejection of Stalinism. The preface to the book alludes to the "guns" of the 1936 purges in the Soviet Union undertaken by Stalin, a prelude to James's interpretation of the Haitian Revolution as the first enactment in the Western world of black revolutionary agency. As noted earlier, James was influenced in this interpretation by Du Bois's interpretation of black self-emancipation from slavery during the Civil War in *Black Reconstruction*. In 1938, James's *A History of Pan-African Revolt* also drew heavily from Du Bois' *Black Reconstruction* to argue that "Africans must win their own freedom."[9] James's book was also influenced by Padmore's 1931 *The Life and Struggles of Negro Toilers*. Cumulatively, Du Bois, Padmore and James reflected a new Pan-African orientation to prize the autonomy and independence of black struggle as part of world revolution.

In 1937, Padmore published *Africa and World Peace*, an attack on the Soviet Union (and the Comintern) for failing to defend Ethiopia from imperialist invasion by Italy. In the same year, he and James established the International African Service Bureau, which in 1938 became the "colonial section" of the Independent Labor Party. The intention was to win people away from Soviet influence and into independent Pan-African struggle. The strategy worked. From 1934, the year of Padmore's Comintern break, to 1945, the Fifth Pan-African Congress, leading members of the anti-colonial left would gravitate to Marxism as a necessary element of the fight for colonial freedom: these would include Kwame Nkrumah of the Gold Coast; Jomo Kenyatta of Kenya; Aime Cesaire of Martinique; Shirley Graham Du Bois from the U.S.; Claudia Jones from Trinidad; Eric Williams of Trinidad and Tobago.

In 1943, during World War II, Du Bois published "The Realities of Africa" in which he criticized world leaders for planning a post-war world without Africa. "One would think that Africa," he wrote, "so important in world trade and world industrial organization and containing at least 125,000,000 people would be carefully considered today in any plan for post-war reconstruction. This does not seem to be the case."[10] Du Bois also complained that the "Atlantic Charter," a plan for the post-war world being drawn up by President Roosevelt and wartime allies, paid no attention to Africa. "If the treatment of Africa in postwar planning begins or ends here the results will be tragic," he wrote.[11] For Du Bois, then, the Pan-African Movement would be a chance for Africans to direct their own place in world history especially in the post-war world.

Critical to the increasing independence of the Pan-African Movement was Stalin's decision to liquidate the Comintern on June 8, 1943 in the name of wartime unity with the imperialist states. The decision was the logical result of the Comintern's own Popular Front political orientation after 1935 which subordinated class struggle to building cross-class alliances in order to defeat fascism. For anti-colonial Marxists like Padmore, the Comintern's liquidation was an opportunity and urgent historical moment for new global leadership in both the struggle against colonialism and the fight for workers' power. It was towards these ends that Padmore formed the Pan-African Federation (PAF) out of the International African Service Bureau.

The PAF set itself with two immediate tasks: to assure that the new Atlantic Charter on "self-determination" would apply to the colonies, and to compel colonial trade unionists to attend the first World Trade Union Conference (WTUC) scheduled for February 1945 in London. The International Labor Organization had formed the WTUC as a successor to the International Federation of Trade Unions, a social-democratic (meaning reformist) alternative to the Communist International. In February 1945, representatives from the Soviet Union and, for the first time in IFTU history, seven delegates from colonial countries, including the British West Indies and British West Africa, met in London.

Padmore saw the WTUC as a recruiting ground to revitalize Pan-African Movement: the PAF made a point to invite West African and Caribbean delegates to the WTUC to meet in Manchester immediately after the conference for the Fifth Pan-African Congress, and the first in 16 years. In fact the Manchester Congress was scheduled on the heels of the WTUC expressly for this purpose, to link labor and the anti-colonial movement more tightly.

Du Bois was himself a distant participant in organizing all of this. Busy in New York City and away from London, Du Bois corresponded with Padmore about plans for a Fifth Congress. Padmore stressed in his letters to Du Bois the importance of African trade unionists being present as a means of proletarianizing the Pan-African Movement.

In April 1945 he wrote to Du Bois that it was "workers and peasants, who must be the driving force behind any movement which we middle-class intellectuals may establish. Today, the African masses, the common people, are awake and not blindly looking to doctors and lawyers to tell them what to do."[12] Padmore's confidence was seemingly confirmed by events of June 1945, which saw the outbreak of a 52-day general strike in Nigeria supported by more than 150,000 workers represented by 17 different unions. On July 15, 1945, the Pan African Federation organized a massive rally in support of the strike at Conway Hall, London, in collaboration with the West African Student Union.[13] Du Bois meanwhile wrote back that he hoped the meeting would include more representatives from Africa than the last Congress.

The same month that Padmore's letter arrived, Du Bois was busy coordinating a Pan-African workshop at the famous Schomburg Collection in Harlem, founded by Puerto Rican activist and archivist Arturo Schomburg. The workshop was part of Du Bois's ongoing effort to build support for his Pan-African organizing from the NAACP. On April 6, the daylong meeting, which included par- ticipation by Francis Nkrumah, wife of the future leader of Ghana, produced a conference declaration. It "called for a democratic China, a free Korea, independence for India and Burma, dominion status for the Gold Coast and Nigeria, and the end of exclusive white rule in Kenya and Rhodesia. Italy would surrender its North African conquests and the territory seized from Ethiopia; Japan would cede Formosa to China."[14] The conference was important for solidifying temporarily NAACP support for Du Bois's Pan-African work as the organization's focus on domestic race relations in the U.S. sometimes clashed with Du Bois's goals of Pan-Africanism. The conference call for a "democratic China" also demonstrated Du Bois's growing support for a Communist victory over the Nationalists.

Meanwhile, in London Padmore led carefully planned efforts to realize a Fifth Pan-African Congress. Organizers stuck to Padmore's intentions to make the meeting representative of a new labor militancy among African workers and peasants. In March, Padmore headed a provisional organizing committee which included a pantheon of African and Caribbean leaders most with trade union backgrounds or roots in mass struggles: Jomo Kenyatta from the Kikuyu Central Association of Kenya; Peter Milliard of British Guiana; Isaac Wallace-Johnson from the West African Youth League of Sierra Leone.

The committee created a "draft manifesto" urging African participation in the upcoming United Nations specifically declaiming an end to the "present system of exploitation" in the colonies and a call for African self-determination. In June, the PAF organized the first All Colonial Peoples Conference in Holborn Town Hall, London. The Conference included 40 delegates, 25 observers, trade unionists and leftist parties and became "something for a dress rehearsal for the Manchester Pan-African Congress."[15] Organizers established a committee tasked to "bring into being as early as possible a 'Colonial International.'"[16] The term indicated the Congress's clear intentions to replace one historical narrative and institution—the 1917 Bolshevik Revolution and the Comintern—with another radically new leadership and vehicle for that leadership.

The aspiration was largely met by careful calculation in planning and carrying out the Manchester conference. At the World Trade Union Council meeting in Paris from September 25 to October 8, the colonial delegates advocated for creation of a "Colonial Council" or "Colonial Department" within the WTUC and for an end of trade union discrimination. They also argued that "the system of colonies is the thin end of the wedge of capitalism, and therefore, the arch enemy of the working class."[17] Representatives such as J.S. Annan, from African labor like the Gold Coast African Railway Employees, who would also be a delegate to the Pan-African Congress, pressed the question of "how . . . to make . . . imperialist governments" responsive to colonial labor. As Annan put it, "Are we to leave these helpless colonial organizations at the mercy of imperialistic capitalism?"[18]

The WTUC stoked the anti-capitalist fires that burst into flame at the Pan-African Congress in Manchester. Du Bois, who flew in a day later for the meeting, was given pride of place. He was unanimously voted by delegates as President of the Congress on its first day. On October 17, Du Bois was formally introduced to the delegates of the meeting by Padmore as the "father of Pan-Africanism." As to the meeting itself, Kwame Nkrumah adequately expressed both its intentions and achievements this way: "We shot into limbo the gradualist aspirations of our African middle classes and intellectuals and expressed the solid down-to-earth will of our workers, trade unionists, farmers and peasants who were decisively represented at Manchester, for independence."[19] Indeed delegates and associations represented at the meeting included the Gold Coast Farmers Association, the Workers League of British Honduras, the Nigerian Trade Unions Congress, the St. Lucia Seamen's and Waterfront Workers' Union. Political organizations present included the African National Congress of South Africa, People's National Party of Jamaica, Grenada Labor Party and the NAACP. Also present were representatives of Asian colonies like the Lanka Sama Samajist Party of Ceylon, indicative of the alliances that would later form the Bandung Conference of Indonesia in 1955.

The Congress program included numerous statements of solidarity expressed to laborers across the colonial world, reports on racism experienced by black soldiers in London, and reports on poverty in the heavily black and Asian East End. Also featured were sessions on "Imperialism in North and West Africa" and reports from the West African Cocoa Farmers Delegation of Gold Coast blaming "British imperialism" for black labor strife.[20] Resolutions were also passed condemning the "systematic exploitation of the economic resources of the West Africa territories" and protesting restrictions on trade unions and lack of enforcement of trade union rights. These labor demands were the material base for resolutions specifically targeting the end of colonization: resolutions called for a removal of British armed forces from Egypt and "full equality of rights for all citizens, without distinction of race, colour and sex" in South Africa—a call for the end of apartheid. Further calls came for recognition of democratic rights of indigenous citizens of Algeria, Tunisia, Morocco, and Libya and an end to French and Italian rule. As Du Bois recorded the final resolution, "We condemn monopoly of capital and rule of private wealth and industry for profit alone. We welcome economic democracy; where, we are going to make the world listen to the facts of our conditions. For their betterment we are going to fight in all and every way we can."[21]

Most significant of all, the congress ended with a "Declaration to the Colonial Workers, Farmers and Intellectuals" written by Kwame

Nkrumah. The Declaration was a precise testament to Padmore's desire for a colonial international that would expressly take the place of the now-defunct Comintern:

> The object of imperialist powers is to exploit. By granting the right to Colonial peoples to govern themselves that Object is defeated ... The Fifth Pan-African Congress therefore calls on the workers and farmers of the Colonies to organize effectively. Colonial workers must be in the front of the battle against Imperialism. Your weapons—the Strike and the Bocyott—are invincible. Today, there is only one road to effective action—the organization of the masses. And in that organization the educated colonials must join. Colonial and Subject Peoples of the World— unite![22]

Nkrumah's "Declaration" must be considered one of the most important political documents of the twentieth century. In one fell swoop it articulated the demands of an emerging and well-organized African movement that in subsequent years would earn major victories in helping bring to an end systems like South African apartheid and the decolonization of Nigeria, Kenya, Sierra Leone and a score of other African states. The Declaration should be seen much like the Communist Manifesto of 1848 on which it was modeled as a document which pushed forward workers struggles across Africa much as the Manifesto had done for Europe.

When he commemorated the Pan-African Congress in his book *Colonial and Coloured Unity: A Program for Action*, a collection of documents from the Manchester conference, George Padmore praised the role of W.E.B. Du Bois in the Congress out of respect for both his lifelong commitment as a founder of Pan-Africanism. In an essay titled "The Pan-African Congress in Perspective," Peter Abrahams acknowledged Du Bois's 1940 book *Dusk of Dawn* as an inspiration for the goals of the Manchester meeting and the establishment of the "Century of the Common Man: Foreword to the Socialist United States of Africa! Long live Pan-Africanism!"[23]

Abraham's cry for a "Socialist United States of Africa" shows us Pan-Africanism's hopes for generating an African version of Marxism customized to African emancipation. Such became the basis, for example, of Julius Nyerere's *Ujamaa* program in Tanzania. Influenced by Maoist conceptions of Marxism grounded in objective national conditions, Nyerere wrote, "It is not part of the job of a socialist . . . to worry about whether or not his actions or proposals are in accordance with what Marx or Lenin wrote . . . The task of a socialist is to think out for himself the best way of achieving desired ends under the conditions which now exist."[24]

In the Gold Coast, after Manchester, Kwame Nkrumah would ascend to become leader of the People's Convention Party and Padmore his closet adviser. Their alliance brought them back into contact with Du Bois over the fate of Ghana's own decolonizing aspirations. Du Bois and Padmore first showed disagreement over the direction liberation should take in a quarrel over Richard Wright's 1955 book *Black Power*, a favorable report on revolutionary prospects in the Gold Coast. Padmore saw the book as another example of the "forward march" of Africa. Du Bois challenged Wright's prescription for African adaptation of Western science and technology (and foreign investment) advocated by Padmore and Nkrumah. "I understand the policy of you and Dr. Nkrumah, although I am a little afraid of it. The power of British and especially American capital once it gets a foothold is tremendous."[25]

Du Bois's skepticism about Western capital's influence on Ghana owed to his lingering and much stronger allegiance than Padmore's to Soviet Communism. Du Bois's views were those of a Cold Warrior perched in anti-Communist America intent on defending the Soviet Union, whereas Padmore was now a Third World expatriate trying to negotiate a "middle ground" between First World capitalism and Second World Communism. For example, in 1944 and 1945 Du Bois frequently used his *Chicago Defender* column "As the Crow Flies" to extol the Soviet Union's role in fighting fascism. During the same period, Padmore's defense of the Soviet Union was limited to support for remnants of its policy of supporting anti-colonial self-determination. In his 1946 book *How Russia Transformed Her Colonial Empire: A Challenge to the Imperialist Powers*, Padmore wrote, "Whatever criticism or charges one might level against Stalin's relation in relation to socialism and world revolution and his programme of 'Socialism in a single country, he has in the main adhered to the fundamental principles laid down by Lenin as far as concerns of the Right of Self-Determination for the Soviet national minorities."[26] Padmore's emphasis here was to distance African anti-colonial struggle from Soviet influence in order to affirm the Pan-African movement's new role as leader in carrying forward the mantle of self-determination struggles.

This difference in perspective would come to a head in Du Bois's review of Padmore's 1956 book *Pan-Africanism or Communism?: The Coming Struggle for Africa*. Padmore wrote that Pan-Africanism intended to "fulfill the socio-economic mission of Communism, under a libertarian political system." Padmore's formula was a combination of state capitalism and Africanist nationalism: "Economically and socially, Pan-Africanism subscribes to the fundamental objectives of democratic-socialism, with state control of the basis of production and distribution."[27] Padmore here eschews proletarian internationalism for a nationalism, as the Indian Marxist M.N. Roy once called it, "painted red." Ironically, given his criticism of Stalinism, Padmore's model of state control of an economy rather than workers' control is actually closer to Stalinism than Socialism from below. Indeed, Padmore's friend Daniel Guerin would tell Padmore that his book had confused Stalinism with Marxism. Padmore's plan also allowed for Western investment and influence on Ghanaian development.

Du Bois's rejection of Padmore's conception was sharp and intended to recuperate the Soviet Union as a mentor for African liberation:

> How can a national African socialism meet the danger of a rising black bourgeoisie associated closely with foreign investors? Padmore wants "an American Marshall Plan" for Africa; he welcomes British capital for the Volta dam. He thinks the Philippines are free. This seems to be dangerous thinking . . .
>
> [W]ith a mass of sick, hungry and ignorant people, led by ambitious young men, like those today supporting tribalism on the Gold Coast and Big Business in Liberia, under skies clouded by foreign investing vultures armed with atom bombs—in such a land, the primary fight is bound to be between private Capital and Socialism, and not between Nationalism and Communism. It may

be in Africa, as it was in Russia, that Communism will prove the only feasible path to Socialism.[28]

Du Bois's warning about rising nationalist elites sounds like the anti-colonial radical Frantz Fanon's historical caution about a "new class"—a national bourgeoisie—which may carry out the historic mission of counter-revolution or "neo-colonialism" after decolonization[29]—a warning that would prove prophetic, as we shall see. Du Bois's dire concerns about Western investment as a ruination of African independence stemmed from direct anger at U.S. support for and investment in apartheid regimes in South Africa and intensive efforts to capitalize other African states like Liberia through natural resource extraction and exploitation of black labor.

At the same time, the Du Bois–Padmore dispute shows numerous shadows of Stalinism. In effect, Padmore and Du Bois were drawn into a dispute over the meaning of Socialism because of Stalinism's very distortions of its meanings. For example, Padmore's support for a "libertarian" approach to Communism reflected anxieties about associating with a corrupted model of Soviet Communism. Du Bois's response, written and published ironically six days *after* Khrushchev's secret speech on Stalin's crimes, also invokes uncritically a disfigured Soviet state bureaucracy as the possible model for Ghana's true liberation. The debate shows how Stalinism had distorted discussions of working-class self-emancipation into narrow frameworks both in their own way beholden to a nationalist conception of "Socialism in One Country." Stalinism's own errors in supporting anti-colonial struggle—the abandonment of Ethiopia and Libya, Popular Front alliance with the imperialist West, the dissolution of the Comintern—were all stepping-stones both to Padmore's rejection of Communist-state support in Ghana and to Du Bois's hardheaded attempt to go against the grain of history by supporting a Stalinist Soviet Union.

Yet because of his absolute commitment to African independence, Du Bois remained aligned to it, at times adapting his stance to the ongoing Cold War. Thus, after 1956, Du Bois began another reassessment of African decolonization. As rapacious U.S. investment in African colonies increased after World War II along with support for South African apartheid, and inspired by China's post-revolution example of nominal support for African liberation, Du Bois deepened his defense of Nkrumah's Ghanaian revolution in particular. As Kevin Gaines notes, many African-American leftists including Maya Angelou, Amiri Baraka, Shirley Graham Du Bois (who married W.E.B. in 1952) and Du Bois himself traveled to Ghana to discuss ways to link Africa's decolonization to African-American freedom struggles. In 1957, Du Bois was forced to decline an invitation to Ghana because of the U.S. revocation of his passport in 1952 after allegations of working as an "agent of a foreign enemy" for his work in the peace movement. In declining, Du Bois wrote to Nkrumah that "when Ghana arises from the dead and faces this modern world" it must "avoid subjection to and ownership of foreign capitalists" and

> Should try to build socialism founded on old African communal life, rejecting the exaggerated private initiative of the West, and seeking to ally itself with the social program of the Progressive Nations; with British and Scandanavian Socialism, with the progress toward the Welfare State in India, Germany, France and the United States; and with the Communist States like the Soviet Union and China, in peaceful cooperation and without presuming to dictate also how Socialism must or can be attained at particular times and places.[30]

Du Bois here imagines Africa as part of a democratic-socialist United Front resonant of the *Panscheel*, or "peaceful cooexistence" doctrines of Jawaharlal Nehru and of efforts by Third World countries to navigate a path between the "first" capitalist world and "second" Socialist World during the Cold War. Du Bois's idea of socialism founded on "old African communal life" reflects an interest in pre-capitalist African societies he explored in his 1915 book *The Negro* and his 1946 book *The World and Africa*. These societies were inspirations for his interest in cooperative economics as well. Remaining constant is Du Bois's admonition to refuse support for advanced capitalist and imperialist states like the U.S.

In 1958, after the return of his passport, Du Bois was again invited by Nkrumah to Ghana, along with his wife Shirley Graham

Du Bois. The invitation was to attend and speak at the All-Colonial Peoples Conference. This time he declined due to poor health. Du Bois was exhausted by travel to Eastern Europe and Tashkent. He was now 90 years old. Instead, Shirley Graham instead went in Du Bois's place and read a speech he had prepared for the event. The speech was titled "The Future of All Africa Lies in Socialism." In it, he again attempted to weld together his support for Pan-Africa and Soviet Communism. He encouraged conference representatives to draw upon long histories of African liberation struggle dating to the Ashanti Wars against Britain while also counseling that Africa's bond was with the "white world . . . closest to those like the Union of Soviet Socialist Republics . . . no mere color of skin but the deeper experience of wage slavery and contempt."[31]

What are we to make of Du Bois's struggle over "Pan Africanism" or "Socialism"? Beginning with the Pan-African movement of 1900, Du Bois asserted African liberation as one of the pillars of his political life and work. He lived to see the decolonization not just of Ghana but Nigeria, Algeria and a score of other African and Asian nations, testament to the scope and scale of the Pan-African movement and its influence on the world. It can thus be said without exaggeration that Du Bois did more to educate African-Americans and people of the African diaspora about Africa than any other person in U.S. history. Black Panther Party leaders like Eldridge Cleaver and Huey P. Newton took direct inspiration from Du Bois in linking black freedom struggles in the U.S. to African decolonization. As Du Bois himself wrote in 1958, "The rise of Africa in the last 15 years has astonished the world. Even the most doubting of American Negroes have suddenly become aware of Africa and its possibilities and particularly of the relation of Africa to the American Negro."[32] Du Bois "opened up" Africa as a companionate space for political freedom struggle for African-Americans. In short, Du Bois's Pan-African scholarship and activism may be considered to be one of the greatest single political successes of his distinguished life.

Du Bois's struggle to see a Socialist Africa brought mixed results. The experiments with Marxist ideas by anti-colonial leaders from Kwame Nkrumah to Julius Nyerere to the African National Congress helped produce successful independence movements often guided generally by Socialist principles. Yet as writers like Ali Mazri and Abdul Babu have shown, formal decolonization also opened the door for new African dependency on western capital and "neocolonial" regimes. "African Socialism" was beset by profoundly uneven economic development within and across Africa and in relationship to the advanced capitalist states. Trade with the Soviet Union and China replaced strict dependency on western states but did not ameliorate other forms of inequality and vulnerability. Du Bois himself predicted much of this. In 1949, in an article for the *National Guardian* entitled "Watch Africa," Du Bois wrote "Today there are signs of an international conspiracy to make the countries of Africa the slums of the world; to steal their land and materials and get power of life and death over millions of blacks.[33]

Finally, Stalinism, and Du Bois's often uncritical attachment to it, shadowed his own dream that "The Future of All Africa Lies in Socialism," the title of one of his late essays. The legacy of Comintern errors in support for African decolonization charted earlier fed skepticism among African leaders like Nyerere in Tanzania about the Soviet Union as mentor and role model. The Stalinization of China's own revolution after 1949, to be discussed in a future chapter, misshaped movements like *Ujaamma* away from workers' control of society. The downfall of regimes like Nkrumah's in Ghana can be attributed to corruptions and repressions of workers' democracy learned from the Stalinized Soviet example. In the end, then, "Pan-Africanism or Socialism" reflected both successes, contradictions and failures in the world revolutionary left's efforts to defeat capitalism and end colonial rule.

PART III

REVOLUTION AND THE COLD WAR, 1945–63

7

Wrestling with the Cold War, Stalinism, and the Blacklist

The "Cold War" officially began in 1946. Winston Churchill gave his famous "iron curtain" speech on March 5, 1946 at Westminster College proclaiming Communism a totalitarian line separating the free capitalist West from the Communist countries. U.S. President Harry Truman declared that the United States government would no longer recognize future Communist states. Josef Stalin, the premier of the Soviet Union, declared that Communism and capitalism were incompatible. The use of atomic weapons by the United States in Hiroshima and Nagasaki began the nuclear arms race between the U.S. and Soviet Union.

For Du Bois, 1946 was also a momentous year and induction into the last stage of his life, lived by and large as an enemy of the American state. This period of Du Bois's life is his most contentious, difficult and, for some, tragic. The man who had built up a reputation as the greatest race leader and African-American intellectual of the twentieth century found himself indicted by the U.S., blacklisted, and dishonored even by longtime allies for his persistent public support for the idea of socialism both within America and in its Cold War nemesis states, China and the Soviet Union in particular.

We can best understand this period of Du Bois's life as a dialectical continuation of everything that came before it. From the moment of his first attendance at Social Democratic Party meetings in Berlin in the 1890s, to his visit to the Soviet Union in 1926, to his public insistence in 1940 that he believed socialism was the answer, the "late" period of Du Bois's life was in many ways a culmination of commitment to the destruction of capitalism, the emancipation of the working class, and the liberation of all minority and colonial peoples.

But this commitment came with a dear and heavy price. Particularly heavy in this period is damage accrued to his reputation from unwavering public support for Stalin, a man who, even within the ranks of the left, had been largely discredited. The 1939 Stalin–Hitler non-aggression pact, for example—a promise by both parties that they would not invade the other during World War II (broken by the Nazis in 1941)—sent hundreds of members of the Communist Party U.S.A. tumbling from party ranks. Further dismay with the direction of Soviet Communism came for some on the radical left when the Communist Party supported a "no-strike pledge" for American workers during World War II to prop up national unity and protect the Soviet Union.

Yet Du Bois, increasingly convinced that the United States was the world's rising imperialist power, was moved further to support for the Soviet Union in response. As well, nominal, continuing Soviet support for colonial independence kept Du Bois's loyalty. Finally, the continuing levels of racism in the U.S. that made the Civil Rights movements necessary were for Du Bois reminders of the absence of racism he had encountered in the Soviet Union in 1926 and 1936.

In 1946, W.E.B. Du Bois further declared his public support for Communism. He traveled to Columbia, South Carolina, at the invitation of Esther Cooper Jackson to give a keynote address at the Southern Negro Youth Congress (SNYC). The Congress was a Communist organization fighting to improve the lives of black southerners. Du Bois's close friend Paul Robeson and the Communist Party member and popular novelist Howard Fast were featured speakers on the program.

Du Bois's speech, "Behold the Land," linked the fate of African-Americans to African diasporic people fighting for their freedoms in the West Indies and Africa as well as to "white slaves of modern capitalistic society."[1] The same year, Du Bois published the essay "Common Objectives" in *Soviet Russia Today*. Du Bois called African-Americans "victims of human slavery and the colonial system" who should sympathize with the attempt by the Soviet Union to eliminate "race and class discrimination." Du Bois also called the Soviet Union "the most hopeful country on earth."[2]

At nearly the same time, the notorious House Committee on Un-American Activities (HUAC) was made a permanent standing committee of the federal government. The committee had been formed in 1938 to investigate possible Nazi ties in the U.S. By the end of World War II it existed to identify and root out Communists in the United States. In 1947, the Committee conducted investigations into Communism in Hollywood. It created the "Hollywood 10" list of screenwriters and directors who were officially "blacklisted" meaning they could not be hired for work because of their membership in the Communist Party or Communist sympathies. HUAC was also an extension of attempts by the federal government to monitor radicalism among African-Americans in particular. During World War II, J. Edgar Hoover and the FBI had created "RACON," a project to monitor activities by African-Americans during the war. The FBI also kept extensive files on African-American writers associated with the left during the war, including Du Bois.[3] Both of these initiatives foreshadowed the later development of "Cointelpro," the Counter Intelligence program that during the 1960s infiltrated black radical organizations like the Black Panthers, and provided information which led to the assassination by the state of movement leaders like Panther Fred Hampton in Chicago.

In 1948, Du Bois was dismissed by the NAACP as Director of Special Research. The NAACP leader Walter White was himself part of what historian Manning Marable calls the "left wing of McCarthyism."[4] The NAACP also severed ties with the Communist front Civil Rights Congress and expelled communist members from its own ranks. Du Bois had struggled against anti-Communism in the NAACP throughout his tenure. When he left the organization he was offered the position of Vice-Chairman of the Council on African Affairs (CAA). The CAA was organized in London in 1939 headed up by Max Yergan and Paul Robeson with participation by Communists like Alpheus Hunton. The group originated to support black Africans living under South African apartheid and striking workers in West Africa. When the CAA was put on the U.S. Attorney General's list of possibly "subversive" organizations, Yergan turned coat, publically attacked Communists, and the Council was put under further scrutiny by the federal government. Du Bois's acceptance of the position as Vice-Chairman put him under closer examination by the federal government and helped lead to his indictment in 1951.

In August, 1949, Du Bois attended an all-Soviet peace conference in Moscow, part of his commitment to ending the production and use of nuclear weapons. Du Bois's speech attacked the United States for its history of exploiting slave labor. He railed against "private corporate wealth" which has "throttled democracy" and been made possible by the "color cast" after the Civil War and Reconstruction.[5] Du Bois also debunked efforts by the United States to claim that capitalism and democracy were superior to Communism: "today in the United States," Du Bois wrote, "organized wealth owns the press and chief news gathering organs and is exercising increased control over the schools and making public discussion and even free thinking difficult and often impossible."[6] Du Bois was clearer than ever that some kind of socialism was the answer: "The cure for this and the way to change the socially planned United States into a welfare state is for the American people to take over the control of the nation in industry as well as government."[7]

1949 was a particularly frigid year in the Cold War, and Du Bois did not go unscathed. His dear friend Paul Robeson was called the "Black Stalin" by Manning Johnson for making pro-Soviet remarks at the World Partisans for Peace Conference in Paris that year. Johnson had been a member of the Communist Party in the 1930s; he later testified against Communism before HUAC. On October 14, 1949, twelve members of the Communist Party were found guilty under the notorious Smith Act (passed in 1940 to force Communists and other radicals to declare their political affiliations) of trying to overthrow the U.S. government. Two months earlier, Du Bois was called to testify before the House Committee on Foreign Relations. He asked whether Americans were right to fear a largescale attack by the Soviet Union. Du Bois replied: "We did not believe this when we asked ten million Russians to die in order to save the world from Hitler. We did not believe it when we begged Russian help to conquer Japan . . . We did want to rule Russia and we cannot rule Alabama"[8]—a reference to ongoing segregation and black resistance to segregation.

Du Bois's personal life was also jolted in 1950 when Nina Gomer Du Bois passed away. Typically, Du Bois did not make much of her passing in his public life. Much of the scholarship on Du Bois suggests that Nina never fully recovered emotionally from the death of their first son, Burghardt. In his own writings, Du Bois intimated that part of Nina died with their son. She is buried in Great Barrington next to him. Nina and Du Bois also endured something of a scandal around Yolande's life: in 1928, she had married the well-known Harlem Renaissance poet Countee Cullen in a high-profile marriage of black intellectual royalty. In 1930, the couple divorced amidst rumors of Cullen's homosexual relationship with a friend. Cullen was in fact gay. After the marriage Yolande remarried and bore the Du Boises a grandchild in 1932. Nina remained close to Yolande throughout, dedicated mainly to family. Yolande could be described as a steadfast partner who, like many of her age, subordinated her life and career to her husband.

The dropping of two devastating atomic bombs by the United States on Nagasaki and Hiroshima in August 1945 and the slaughter of hundreds of thousands of innocent Japanese citizens immediately ignited peace and disarmament movements in the United States and around the world. Du Bois was compelled to the work for several reasons. One was as a way of fighting against U.S. attempts to characterize the non-Western world and Communist states as the progenitors of violence and to call attention to the United States' role as leading producer (and user) of atomic weapons. To that end he reprinted and circulated the "Stockholm Appeal" to abolish the atomic bomb. Working with other activists, they collected more than two million signatures. The group also issued "Peacegrams" across the country calling for an end to atomic weapons.

A second major reason for Du Bois's peace activism was his commitment to ending war, and imperialist war, as engines of capitalism and the Cold War fight against socialism. As he put it in a speech he often recited to audiences across the country:

When, then, modern world revolution started of which that of Russia is but a part, revolution which has changed the face of industry in every modern nation, here in America there has started a desperate effort to lead this nation into witchhunting and world war, to stop this world trend toward abolition of labor exploitation and a real brotherhood of man, and to abolish forever the vulgar role of private wealth. Thus the Peace movement epitomizes in itself the world uplift today and of this the American Negroes must become increasingly aware if they do not want to fall behind progress and hold back the march of mankind.[9]

Du Bois found an immediate ally in this work in Shirley Graham. Graham was born in Indianapolis, Indiana, and attended Oberlin College, one of the first U.S. colleges to admit women and African-American students. Graham had first met Du Bois in 1936. She was then an activist, practicing playwright and aspiring actress. Du

Van Vechten, Carl, 1880–1964. Shirley Graham Du Bois, July 18, 1946. W.E.B. Du Bois Papers (MS 312). Special Collections and University Archives, University of Massachusetts Amherst Libraries

Bois had published an article by her on African-American music in *The Crisis* not long after they met. In the 1940s, Graham joined the all-women group Sojourners for Truth and Justice. The group's member militated against both domestic violence against women and global violence in the form of war. The group's named derived from the legendary ex-slave, abolitionist and feminist Sojourner Truth. She also served for a time as a contributing editor to the Communist journal *Masses & Mainstream*. During the 1930s and 1940s she wrote a number of plays, radio scripts, and in the 1950s, autobiographies of prominent African-American leaders like Frederick Douglass and Phyllis Wheatley, the first African-American to publish a book of poems in the United States.

Graham's own allies and friends included Claudia Jones and other black women in the Communist Party. Graham denied being a member of the Party, but was very supportive of its work. Jones, from Trinidad, was a major theoretician on women's oppression in the Communist Party. She would become friends and companions to both Shirley and W.E.B. In 1949, Graham attended the World Peace Conference in Paris as did Paul Robeson. She also played a role at the World Congress for Peace at the Waldorf Astoria Hotel in New York in 1950, which Du Bois likewise attended. Graham emphasized in her activism the special role of women: "Unless women everywhere come out very strong in the struggle for peace selfish men are going to drag us into war. And the heaviest responsibility lies on the women of America. We are the only women in the world who have not suffered horribly in wars."[10]

A short time later Graham offered to assist Du Bois with his own political organizing work as a secretary. In 1951 they were married. There is little question that Graham Du Bois encouraged Du Bois not only in his peace activism but in his public support for Communism and revolutions in China and the Soviet Union. She would remain with Du Bois to the end of his days, and outlive him as an activist to the end of her own.[11] Together they would have a son, David Graham Du Bois. In the 1960s, after her husband's death, Graham Du Bois would continue her career as an employee of the state in Ghana in support of Nkrumah's government, as a citizen-advocate in Egypt

W.E.B. Du Bois and Paul Robeson World Peace Congress in Paris, April 20, 1949. W.E.B. Du Bois Papers (MS 312). Special Collections and University Archives, University of Massachusetts Amherst Libraries

under Nasser, and later a proponent of the Cultural Revolution in China, where she is buried.[12]

In 1950, Du Bois joined the Peace Information Center, a U.S. group coordinating activities against atomic weapons. In the same year, the United States sent troops to South Korea to fight against a putatively Communist North Korea (with China as its ally). Korea had been partitioned at the end of World War II after years of Japanese occupation. The war became a focal-point of Cold War anti-Communism, and anti-war protests were attacked by the government as un-American and pro-Communist. The state in turn attacked the peace movement as un-American and pro-Communist. U.S. Secretary of State Dean Acheson was quoted in the *New York Times* as saying that the Stockholm Appeal "should be recognized for what it is—a propaganda trick in the spurious 'peace offensive' of the Soviet Union."[13] Du Bois responded on behalf of the Peace Information Center:

Today in this country it is becoming standard reaction to call anything "communist" and therefore subversive and unpatriotic, which anybody for any reason dislikes. We feel strongly that this tactic has already gone too far; that it is not sufficient today to trace a proposal to a communist source to dismiss it with contempt . . . Regardless of our other beliefs and affiliation, we are united in the organization for the one and only purpose of informing the American people on the issues of peace.[14]

Despite government hostility, Du Bois refused to back off. He traveled to Prague for another peace conference and accepted an invitation to run for the United States Senate on the American Labor Party ticket. This was a left-wing electoral formation created in New York state in the late 1930s, supported by U.S. Communists and others. Its greatest achievement had been the recurrent election to Congress of Vito Marcantonio. Du Bois joined him and the candidate for governor, John T. McManus, editor of the left-wing weekly *National Guardian*. The ticket was swamped in the anti-Communist tide. Out of five million votes, Du Bois got 205,000, yet he saw this as support to be "counted for peace and civil rights," adding: "For this I was happy."[15] Again in 1956, a presidential election year, Du Bois declared in *The Nation*, "I shall not go to the polls. I have not registered. I believe that democracy has so far disappeared in the United States that no 'two evils' exist. There is but one evil party with two names, and it will be elected despite all I can do or say. There is no third party."[16] Du Bois's cynicism towards the two-parties had hardened because of their joint support of the Cold War, of anti-Communism, of repression of political dissent, and of failure to achieve any significant gains for African-Americans. Yet in 1957, hailing a civil rights demonstration of 27,000 in Washington, D.C., he would urge (in an article written for the *National Guardian*): "Watchword for Negroes: Register and Vote!" Noting the potential power of the new movement—which protested "against lawlessness and discrimination" and "did not refer to the great parties" of Republicans and Democrats—he envisioned the possibility in the South "of the localities and their voters to seize and hold government."

Not long after Du Bois's Senate campaign the U.S. Justice Department notified the Peace Information Center that it must register with the Department under terms of the Foreign Agents

Registration Act. The letter accused the Center of being a front for the Soviet Union. When the Center refused its members were indicted in February, 1951.

Du Bois's indictment became a *cause célèbre* for friends around the world. An "International Committee in Defense of Dr. W.E.B. Du Bois and his Colleagues" was formed. The Committee included members from France, Belgium, Brazil, the Soviet Union, Hungary, and China. Supporting letters arrived from labor groups like the World Federation of Teachers Unions and the World Federation of Scientific Workers. Alice Citron, a Harlem school teacher, volunteered to help Du Bois plan his defense. Citron had been suspended without pay because she refused to answer the question: "Are you or were you ever a member of the Communist Party?"[17]

Du Bois spoke around the country at rallies in his own defense. He continued to criticize wealth inequality in the United States and "American enterprise that fattens off Central African copper."[18] He also said that "no man can be sure of earning a living, of escaping slander and personal violence" in America unless he proclaims that

He hates Russia.

He opposes socialism and communism.

He supports wholeheartedly the war in Korea.

He is ready to spend any amount for further war; anywhere or anytime.

He is ready to fight the Soviet Union, China and any other country or all

Countries together.

He believes in the use of the atom bomb . . .[19]

Despite his protests and a wide outpouring of public support, Du Bois was put on trial in Washington D.C. After much testimony and several weeks of trial, the judge ruled that the government had "failed to support" its allegations. Du Bois was free in victory. About the government's intimidation tactics Du Bois wrote:

The real object was to prevent American citizens of any sort from daring to think or talk against the determination of big business to reduce Asia to colonial subserviency to American industry; to reweld the chains on Africa; to consolidate United States control of the Caribbean and South America; and above all to crush socialism in the Soviet Union and China. That was the object of this case.[20]

Despite his legal victory, the government's trial and accusations against Du Bois scared away former friends and supporters. Only one of the 50 presidents of Negro colleges which Du Bois knew well and had visited attended a public birthday party for Du Bois in Harlem after he was indicted. Some African-American churches and school teachers shunned him. Du Bois complained that this showed "the wide fear and intimidation of the Negro people of America."[21]

In 1950, Du Bois published a book about his indictment and trial called *In Battle for Peace*. The book was published by the Communist-supported outlet *Masses & Mainstream*. In it he thanked Communists around the world for supporting him. But the blacklisting of Du Bois had begun. Henry Giroux, his publisher, turned down "Russia and America: An Interpretation," his book comparing the histories of the Soviet Union and United States; his mail was tampered with; colleges and universities stopped inviting him to speak. The NAACP would no longer allow local branches to invite him to speak or sponsor his lectures. As Du Bois put it, "The colored children ceased to hear my name."[22]

The blacklisting of W.E.B. Du Bois only inspired him to try to speak out more strongly against anti-Communism in the United States. It also pushed him even further into support of both Joseph Stalin and the Soviet Union and of the Chinese Communist Revolution of 1949. Du Bois felt cornered by a country which proclaimed itself democratic and with a free press but which fired, shunned or silenced critics of that same system. He began to argue more publically that although the Soviet Union had problems, it was in many ways an equal or superior system to democratic capitalism because of its commitment in name to economic equality and anti-racism. He also argued, as did others on the left, that the repression of political voices in the U.S. and especially its racism towards African-Americans delegitimated its claims to be a free country, superior to so-called "totalitarian" Communist states.

This is the main theme of Du Bois's unpublished manuscript "Russia and America." Du Bois submitted it to his publisher in 1950. Giroux rejected it on the grounds that it was too critical of America and took too favorable a view of the Soviet Union. The book combined reports from Du Bois's three trips to the Soviet Union, in 1926, 1936, and in 1949 for attendance at the World Peace Congress. "Russia and America" is a strange and shaggy work. It is Du Bois scrambling at a low point in his political career to provide a justification for his ongoing support for the Soviet Union, while proving to American readers that the Soviet people and American people had histories of common struggle behind them. Du Bois invoked the memory of the American Revolution and the Bolshevik Revolution of 1917 as great examples of popular struggles. He pointed out that the common people of both countries—anti-colonialists in the case of America, peasants and workers in the case of the Soviet Union—had fought to overthrow tyrants. He also argued that the Cold War helped to keep ordinary Americans and Russians divided from each other. Just one year before he wrote "Russia and America," the Soviet Union had successfully conducted its first test of a nuclear weapon. Du Bois worried out loud that World War III might mean the destruction of the citizenship of both countries.

"Russia and America" also argued that Franklin Roosevelt's refusal to include black farm laborers and domestics in its New Deal programs from recovery was a betrayal of African-Americans reminiscent of the federal government's betrayal of the Reconstruction project. "Thus three million Negro workers, more than half of the total who must work for their livelihood, were not covered by the industrial codes. These three million were the backbone of the Negro consumer market."[23] Importantly for Du Bois, the failures of the New Deal were failures of what he calls an "incipient socialism" that had been better realized in the Soviet Union.

"Russia and America" also tendered a defense of the Russian Revolution that weighed its achievements against other revolutions in Western history and the attempts by Western imperial powers to keep Russia underfoot. It is also an attempt to compare it to the African-American freedom struggle which in *Black Reconstruction* he called "an upheaval of humanity like the Reformation and French Revolution."[24]

> We may ask whether or not the Russian Revolution might not have been carried through with less blood and cruelty, with less appeal to brute force. We may believe that with all the gain from the efforts of Lenin and Stalin, most of it might not have been accomplished at lower cost to the decent instincts of mankind. But Russia answers and has right to answer, that this revolution cost less in life and decency than the French Revolution, than the Protestant revolution, and than the English Civil War; that the chief guilt for the high cost of communism was not the fault of Russia but of America and Americans which silently condoned the slavery of Russians for centuries and then at fabulous cost tried for ten years to reenslave them to the degenerate Czars and filthy priesthood. If the cost of revolution was excessive and revolting, the cost is certainly not to rest on Russia alone.[25]

"Russia and America" demonstrated Du Bois's continuing inattention to abuses of Stalinism and Stalin's hijacking of the principles of Marxism and Leninism. For example, Du Bois tried to show that democracy existed in the Soviet Union by pointing out that elections there had high rates of participation. He did not point out the Communist Party was the only party Soviets could reasonably vote for. Du Bois also justified the violent repression of peasants under Stalin during the liquidation of the *kulak*, or small farm system, saying that it had been necessary for advancing the revolution. Du Bois defended the Stalinist "purges" of his political enemies in the 1936 "show trials" by alleging their betrayal of the revolution. Du Bois was especially critical of Leon Trotsky. Trotsky, one-time leader of the Red Army and a close confidant and ally of Lenin during the 1917 Revolution, was accused by Du Bois of conspiring with German fascism to destroy the Russian Revolution. Du Bois uncritically accepted lies told by Stalin to defend his own regime of power and reign of terror.

In 1953 Stalin died. Du Bois's obituary published in the *National Guardian* was extremely flattering. "Joseph Stalin was a great man," he wrote. "He was the son of a serf, but stood calmly before the great without hesitation or nerves."[26] Du Bois also praised Stalin for his three "great decisions." The first was liberating peasants by destroying the kulak system which "clung tenaciously to capitalism."[27] The second was leading the Soviet Union in the fight against fascism during the Second World War. "He risked the utter ruin of socialism in order to smash the dictatorship of Hitler and Mussolini,"[28] wrote Du Bois, indirectly reminding readers that the Soviet Union had sacrificed more than one million lives to win the war. The third was negotiating peace at the end of the war. Here Du Bois praised Stalin for insisting to Western imperialist leaders that the *Cordon Sanitaire* (the protective barrier of territories created by the West after World War I to contain Bolshevism) be returned to the Soviet Union and that the "The Balkans were not to be left helpless before Western exploitation for the benefit of land monopoly. The workers and peasants there must have their say."[29]

Du Bois was referring to the Balkan states (Bulgaria, Macedonia, Albania for example) where after 1945 the Soviet Union supported brutally repressive satellite regimes. His analysis of Stalin failed to mention this fact. Also, Du Bois failed to note the fact the Stalinist regime had collaborated with the imperialist states (France, Britain, the United States) by liquidating the Communist International in 1943 and repressing workers' movements in countries like the United States in the name of winning the war and defending "Socialism in One Country"—the Soviet Union. Similarly, in 1956, when workers in Hungary rebelled against the heavily repressive Soviet-style Communist Party, Du Bois defended the decision of the Soviet Union to smash their rebellion. He argued that the workers were being disloyal to the attempt to build socialism.

Du Bois's Stalinism can be identified as support for a dictatorial, undemocratic regime in which workers were not in command of either the production of goods or the conditions of their own labor. The Soviet bureaucracy served as the ruling elite of the country which extracted wealth and resources from the workers of the nation, a socio-economic formation that some Marxists (including C.L.R. James and the British socialist Tony Cliff) have diagnosed as "state capitalism."[30] This model was followed closely by Soviet satellite states and by Mao Tse-Tung in China. There too, within ten years of the 1949 Communist revolution, the Chinese Communist Party was restricting political dissent, denying free speech, and repressing attempts at workers organizing in their own interests against the state.

Du Bois did not recant his loyalty to Stalin even after Nikita Khrushchev's famous 1956 speech in which he detailed crimes, distortions and lies of the Stalin years of power. Khrushchev acknowledged the famines that had been created by the destruction of the kulaks, the repression of political dissidents under Stalin, and the restrictions of political freedom under his rule. Du Bois did refer to the period of the famine as the "great madness" but also wrote that "the total result was a glorious victory in the uplift of mankind."[31] About Stalin himself Du Bois wrote, "I am fully ready to believe that Stalin was cruel and that there are no doubts that in the Soviet Union there was a place for an excessive suspicion and the cases of persecution of the innocent when tolerance and justice would give more results."[32]

A fair summation of the conflicts expressed in Du Bois's dedication to Stalinism may be that while Du Bois clearly sought to defend principles of socialism and the need for a socialist revolution, this defense was seriously compromised by his silence about, and sometimes defense of, varying features of Stalinist repression. The murderous atrocities of the Stalin regime, and later the Maoist regime, as we shall see, stood in stark contrast to the humane values that Du Bois believed in and to a conception of socialism he himself voices which would allow workers to take control of their society.

In these mistakes Du Bois was like many of his revolutionary contemporaries. The African-American singer Paul Robeson, leaders of African decolonization movements like Kwame Nkrumah, Mao Tse-Tung and others all failed to criticize adequately Stalin's errors. Tragically, these silences did significant damage to the reputation of Communism and Marxism, and help us understand why, during the Cold War and after, Communism was vilified as an ideology in the capitalist world, and why reclaiming the better socialist principles of Du Bois is important to his legacy and the battle for a real socialist society.

It should also be added that Du Bois's socialist commitments were by no means contained by the Stalinist variant of Communism. He sought other outlets for the expression of his perspectives—writing more than a hundred articles for the independent left-wing weekly *National Guardian* and contributing to the independent socialist journal *Monthly Review*. In 1955 he spoke at a centennial anniversary of the birth of Eugene V. Debs, sponsored by these two periodicals, plus *I.F. Stone's Weekly* and the *American Socialist* (a Trotskyist offshoot). Du Bois emphasized: "The socialism of Eugene Debs was founded on the democratic state in which the law of the land was to be determined by the will of the people." In 1958, he justified his support of a new socialist regroupment effort (involving some of the same forces, and also including remnants of the old Progressive Party as well as mainstream Trotskyists of the Socialist Workers Party) with the comment that "Trotsky and Stalin are dead and in probability will remain so," but that the unified forces were agreed on what for him were seven key points: "no more war; cease preparation for war and atomic bomb testing; stop universal military service; justice to labor with fair taxation; abolish the racial and color line; peaceful co-existence with socialist states; recognition of a citizens' right to vote for Socialism." For Du Bois, these were the essentials.[33]

8

The East is Red:
Supporting Revolutions in Asia

> This is a morning when the sunlight is streaming from the East,
> and I mean the East: China and India and Indonesia.
>
> —W.E.B. Du Bois, 1945

The Cold War was built from a triumphalist narrative of American exceptionalism in which the U.S. portrayed itself as a bastion of freedom against Communism. While the Soviet Union was the primary target and nemesis of the U.S. state during the Cold War, China's successful 1949 Communist revolution drew it immediately into the orbit of American hostility. The U.S. had continuously backed the Nationalist Party of Chiang Kai-shek before and during World War II. When civil war broke out between the Nationalists and Communists, the U.S. sided with the Nationalists, and rejected the Communist victory in 1949. The war thus hardened a narrative of American superiority dubbed the "American Century" by magazine publisher Henry Luce, who dedicated pages of his publications *Time* and *Life* magazine to exhorting the U.S. state not to "lose" China into the Communist pantheon. After the end of the war, as the U.S. state was swinging into its Cold War stance, Du Bois was firming up his dedication to the Chinese Communist cause, and extending his support to Asian decolonizing movements across the world. Thus after the return of his U.S. passport in 1958, as soon as he was able, Du Bois made several late-in-life visits to China in support of the Revolution. In his writings on China, Du Bois struggled to accommodate to his thinking the unique role of the peasantry in building a proletarian revolution, and as with his writing on the Soviet Union, generally turned a blind eye towards failures of the Revolution like the Great

Leap Forward. In general, Du Bois's support for China's Communist revolution was a logical extension of his support for the Russian Revolution, his lifelong commitment to colonial self-determination, and his increasing animus towards the chauvinism and militarism of the United States especially in the aftermath of its World War II victory. Thus Du Bois's writings and travels to Asia represent an important chapter and turning point in his political evolution, one which resulted in his further marginalization and demonization in anti-Communist America.

As noted earlier, Du Bois had leapt at the opportunity to visit Japan and China for the first time in 1936. Officially the two countries were at war when he arrived. In the early 1930s, Japan began colonizing parts of China. Du Bois was initially frustrated at the conflict. He felt the two Asian countries represented the potential to challenge the dominance of white Western imperialism. "With China and Japan in rivalry, war and hatred," he wrote, "Europe will continue to rule the world for her own ends."[1]

Thus when World War II broke out, Du Bois wrote that the fate of Asia could determine the fate of the scheme of Western imperialism. "The greatest and most dangerous race problem today is the problem of relations between Asia and Europe: the question as to how far 'East is East and West is West' and of how long they are going to retain the relation of master and serf."[2] Du Bois fundamentally interpreted the war itself as an attempt by the capitalist and colonial states to try and consolidate their hold of colonies in Asia and Africa.

At the same time, Du Bois's deepening analysis of colonialism during the war inspired him to write about the ancient ties between people in Asia and Africa. In 1946, he published his book *The World and Africa*. The book looked at ancient migrations from Africa into Asia and anthropological evidence of exchange between populations:

The Asiatic and African blacks were strewn along a straight path between tropical Asia and tropical Africa, and there was much racial intermingling between Africa and western Asia. In Arabia particularly the Mongoloids and Negroids mingled from earliest times. The Mongoloids invaded North Africa in prehistoric times, and their union with the Negroes formed the Libyans. Later there was considerable commerce and contact between the Phoenicians of North Africa, especially Carthage, and the black peoples of the Sudan.[3]

Du Bois hoped that his scholarship would help inspire solidarity between peoples of African and Asian descent.

World War II was also a turning point in Du Bois's analysis of Asian imperialism. Japan's invasion of Nanjing in 1937 had begun to erode his long-time support for that country as a 'rising' power in Asia. During the war Japanese brutalities in China, Korea, Burma, and the Philippines earned Du Bois's denunciations as an imitator of Western imperialist methods. When he wrote his final *Autobiography* in the late 1950s, Du Bois excluded Japan from his pantheon of nations where he hoped socialism might flourish. From the Japanese example Du Bois also understood that "colored" capitalism would not be an alternative to capitalism and that imperialism by any country could not be excused or tolerated.

Du Bois's turn to a more radical interpretation of Asia's role in World War II was also prompted by American support for the Kuomintang (Nationalist) Party in its civil war with the Chinese Communist Party for control of the country. Du Bois felt that the United States wanted the Nationalist Party to win only because its leader Chiang Kai-shek would serve American interests more than the Communists. Du Bois was thus upset that Chiang Kai-shek's wife, Madame Chiang Kai-shek, was paraded around the United States as a celebrity who tried to convince Americans not to support Communism in China. "It is time," he wrote, "that Public Opinion . . . refuse to be stampeded by the silly yell of 'Communist' and try to give the great and long suffering Chinese people a chance to have real voice in their own government."[4]

Du Bois also felt that the U.S. government feared a Chinese victory because it might convince African-Americans that socialism was superior to capitalism. "White America fears that the example of the Soviet Union and China may tempt the Negroes of America to see the salvation in socialism rather than in the free enterprise of capitalism."[5]

In 1948, Du Bois spoke at a national conference organized by the Committee for a Democratic Far Eastern Policy. The Committee was largely a Communist front group chaired by Maud Russell in New York. Among the members of the Committee was long-time China advocate Agnes Smedley, author of several books on China and for a brief time in Shanghai a spy working on behalf of the Soviet Union. Smedley would eventually be driven from America by the Cold War and die in Beijing a national hero.

At the 1948 meeting, Du Bois condemned U.S. support for Kuomintang leader Chiang Kai-shek.[6] In the same year, inspired by India's declaration of independence, Du Bois wrote hopefully that "Asia is disappearing as a colonial area" and that "China is beating Chiang Kai-shek, puppet of the West, to his knees."[7]

During the 1940s, Du Bois also remained a steadfast supporter of India's independence struggle. Du Bois wrote letters to both Nehru and Gandhi praising their efforts to lead the country to freedom. Du Bois shared and was influenced by Nehru's writings on Indian liberation, especially his argument that India had an historical destiny to become an independent nation. Du Bois thought the argument suitable to struggles of African-Americans and that Nehru spoke for oppressed peoples and nations everywhere in his writings on India. Du Bois also called August 15, 1947, the "greatest historical date of the nineteenth and twentieth centuries." ". . . [F]or on that date four hundred million colored folk of Asia were loosed from the domination of the white people of Europe."[8] He praised Gandhi as one of the greatest leaders of the twentieth century, and noted favorably Gandhi's influence on Martin Luther King, Jr., during his non-violent bus boycott campaigns in the U.S.

Du Bois's single disappointment with Indian independence was that it came with the partition of India and Pakistan, one majority Hindu, the other Muslim. Du Bois saw the partition as a legacy of British colonial rule and its attempts to divide the country along religious lines. Du Bois also tended to blame Muhammad Ali Jinnah, founder and President of the All-India Muslim League which fought for Muslim sovereignty including partition. Jinnah pushed for and won passage of the 1940 Lahore Resolution which paved the way for partition. After partition he became the first Governor-General of Pakistan. Du Bois's unfair characterization of Jinnah as a divider of national unity in India reveals his overwhelming desire and dashed hopes for a united India.

Du Bois was also temporarily upset with Indian Prime Minister Jawaharlal Nehru after independence when he began to jail Communists opposed to his ruling Indian National Congress Party. Du Bois shunned Nehru when he visited the United States in 1952. But later during the Civil Rights era, Du Bois took inspiration from India's successful liberation struggle. In 1956, Du Bois wrote to Nehru "We are not yet equal citizens, but conditions are improving and real emancipation is in sight. For this we have to thank the rise of the Soviet Republics and the rise and growth of free India."[9] He also wrote that African-Americans should take special inspiration from India's successful freedom struggle as a blow against racism. "American Negroes, particularly," he wrote, "have every reason to hail the new and free India . . . The sun of the colored man has arisen in Asia and it will yet rise in Africa and America and the West Indies."[10]

In 1957, Du Bois wrote "The American Negro is not yet free" and that "real human equality and brotherhood in the United States will come only under the leadership of another Gandhi."[11] When Martin Luther King Jr. led civil rights activists in Montgomery, Alabama in non-violent civil disobedience Du Bois praised him as a man "who had read Hegel, knew of Karl Marx, and had followed Mohandas Karamchand Gandhi."[12]

Du Bois was also horrified at the U.S. use of atomic weapons to end World War II and the racism it directed against Asian people both at home and abroad. Du Bois saw World War II as a "race war" directed against non-white people in Asia and Africa. In 1941, when the U.S. government interned hundreds of thousands of Japanese in "concentration camps" across the west and southwest in the name of war-time security, Du Bois encouraged readers of the African-American press to protest the blatant racism and discrimination. He expressed outrage at the U.S. bombing of Hiroshima and Nagasaki in August, 1945 which resulted in the deaths of hundreds of thousands of Japanese civilians.

Thus after the dropping of the atomic bombs on Japan, Du Bois threw himself into peace activism wholesale. He took part in the Cultural and Scientific Conference for World Peace at the Waldorf-

Astoria Hotel in New York in March of 1949. Because representatives from the Soviet Union were present, the meeting was attacked by the *New York Times* as one of the "most controversial meetings in recent New York history,"[13] another sign of the Cold War. Du Bois protested anti-Communist bias at his speech at the meeting: "This conference was not called to defend communism nor socialism nor the American way of life. It was called to promote peace!"[14] In 1950, Du Bois wrote, "We have to live in the world with Russia and China. If we worked together with the Soviet Union against the menace of Hitler, can we not work with them at a time when only faith can save us from utter atomic disaster?"[15]

Du Bois also publically supported Indonesians in their fight for independence from colonial Dutch rule from 1947 to 1949 which resulted in recognition of the Indonesian Republic. "So today we have a great nation of brown people, new to the world and struggling with new and intricate problems. These problems are the world old problems of how they may eat and drink and be sheltered and yet not be slaves to their work and slaves to other folks who get riches from their work."[16] Du Bois also celebrated Burma's independence from British colonial rule in 1948. In 1950, he wrote in support of the revolt against British colonial rule in Malaya (Maylasia). Each of these victories in his mind was a blow against white supremacy and imperialism.

At the same time, the Holocaust against Jews in Hitler's Germany made Du Bois skeptical about the prospects for a world "without racial conflict."[17] About World War II he wrote, "The supertragedy of this war is the treatment of Jews in Germany. There has been nothing comparable to this in modern history. Yet its technique and its reasoning have been based upon a race philosophy similar to that which has dominated both Great Britain and the United States in relation to colored people."[18]

In 1948, Du Bois wrote an impassioned appeal for the United Nations to approve the formation of the State of Israel in an essay called "The Case for the Jews." Du Bois saw Jewish people as an oppressed minority subject to thousands of years of Western racism and later colonialism, like other Africans and Asians. Like many of his contemporaries on the left, he did not recognize the indigenous

Palestinian population in his support for a Jewish state. Robin D.G. Kelley has aptly summarized this contradictory viewpoint in explaining why African-Americans on the left like Du Bois supported Israel and neglected Palestinians:

> There is the convergence of Israel's Zionists roots—a nationalist ideology generated partly in opposition to racist/ethnic/religious oppression, but also motivated by an imperative to bring modernization to a so-called backward Arab world—and the post-Ottoman colonial domination of the region by Britain and France. Ultimately this convergence put Jewish settlers in conflict with British imperialism. The nationalist and anticolonial character of Israel's war of independence camouflaged its own colonial project.[19]

Du Bois's view of Israel began to change in 1956 when it joined France and England in an attempt to seize the Suez Canal from Egypt. Du Bois began to recognize Israel as aligned clearly with the imperialist West.

China's successful Communist revolution of 1949, under the leadership of Mao Tse-Tung was for Du Bois the most important event in Asia after India's independence. Du Bois's enthusiasm for China's revolution was stoked by his friend Agnes Smedley. As noted earlier Smedley was an American working-class woman who moved to China during the early 1930s and wrote several books in support of the Communist Party in its fight against the Kuomintang. Smedley spoke alongside Du Bois at the 1949 World Peace conference. Accused of being a Communist, she left the U.S. and died in Beijing. Du Bois too wanted to travel to China after its 1949 revolution, but could not because his passport had been revoked in 1952 when he was arrested and accused of being a "foreign agent" for the Soviet Union for his peace work.

In 1955, leaders of 29 decolonizing countries, including Zhou Enlai, Prime Minster of China, met in Bandung, Indonesia to express their joint struggle. Du Bois was prevented from attending the conference because of the revocation of his passport. However, he supported the meeting from a distance. The meeting was significant for marking growing support by African-American intellectuals for Asian anti-colonial movements. The novelist Richard Wright, living in exile in Paris, traveled to Bandung and wrote a book about the event in support of Afro-Asian unity titled *The Color Curtain*. New York Congressman Adam Clayton Powell, Jr., also attended the meeting.

In 1956, China officially invited Du Bois to visit and lecture but he still could not gain permission from the U.S. to travel. The United States government did not want a prominent African-American like Du Bois to visit its Cold War enemies in support for Communism. In 1958, Du Bois's passport was returned to him. In 1959, Chinese cultural minister Kuo Mo-jo and Madame Soong Ching-ling renewed the invitation to visit. China's Communist Party knew Du Bois to be a public supporter of the revolution and wanted to feature Du Bois's support for the revolution as part of its propaganda war with the U.S. Du Bois was also keen to go to demonstrate to other Americans, and African-Americans, the importance of international solidarity among oppressed peoples. "I wanted to re-visit China because it is a land of colored people"—a statement reflecting the "Bandung Spirit" of the era.[20]

Du Bois arrived in Beijing in February 1959 from Moscow. He saw the trip as a chance to know for himself whether Western Cold War propaganda was right or whether socialism could succeed: "Fantastic tales of the failure of Socialism and the impossibility of communism fill our periodicals and books. Most Americans today are convinced that Socialism has failed or will fail in the near future . . . We are here to learn the facts in this crisis of modern civilization."[21]

Du Bois came away convinced that China's revolution was succeeding. In Beijing, he was astonished by the city of six million people, "its hard workers" a symbol to Du Bois of the success of China's proletarian revolution. Looking out from his hotel window Du Bois nearly gasped at the level of progress since his last visit in 1959: "We saw the planning of a nation and a system of work rising over the entrails of dead empire."[22]

One reason for his optimistic view was that Du Bois's visit was carefully managed by Chinese leadership. He was given no insight into the failures of China's Great Leap Forward, a disastrous experiment in rural development that had resulted in the starvation of millions of Chinese in the immediate years preceding his visit. Instead, he was escorted more than 5,000 miles through Shanghai, Canton (now Guangzhou), Chungking, Chengdu and Nanjing, site of the 1937 Japanese massacre. He also toured schools and colleges and visited with China's "minority groups," Muslims and other people who were not part of the "Han" majority population. These visits were intended to demonstrate the social harmony produced by the revolution.

Du Bois's 91st birthday was celebrated in stately ceremonial style. He spoke at a rally in Tiananmen Square to an adoring audience who perceived him as an American friend of the revolution. Du Bois used the speech to celebrate the accomplishments of the revolution and to urge African countries to follow the example of China. Du Bois was deeply moved by the show of Chinese affection: "we who all our lives have been liable to insult and discrimination on account of our race and color, in China have met universal goodwill and love, such as we never expected."[23]

Du Bois also made clear that China's revolution should be a beacon to the rest of the world's oppressed: "Speak, China, and tell your truth to Africa and to the world. What people have been despised as you have? Who more than you have been rejected of men? . . . Tell this to Africa, for today Africa stands on new feet, with new eyesight, with new brains and asks: 'Where am I and why?'"[24]

Du Bois also held a four-hour meeting with Chinese Communist Party Chairman Mao Tse-Tung and Prime Minister Zhou Enlai. The meeting took place at Mao's villa in Wuhan in central China. Du Bois demonstrated U.S. racism to the Chairman by insisting that "Many of my family have been exterminated."[25] Mao in turn said that a man's "only mistake is to lie down and let the enemy walk over him," telling Du Bois, "This, I gather, you have never done. You have continued the struggle for your people, for all the decent people of America."[26]

Also present at the meeting with Mao was the American writer Anna Louise Strong. Strong had become a radical during the World War I era in Seattle, especially during its General Strike, before moving to Russia then China in support of revolutions in both countries. Du Bois counted her as a friend especially after they were both criticized severely by the U.S. government during the Cold War for their support for Communist revolutions.

Du Bois's tour across China confirmed his view that working people were happy and in charge of their lives in China. "The people of the land I saw: the workers, the factory hands, the farmers and laborers, scrubwomen and servants . . . and always I saw a happy people; people with faith that needs no church or priest, and who laugh gaily when the Monkey King overthrows the angels."[27] (The Monkey King is the hero of the Ming Dynasty novel *Journey to the West* who rallies his friends to defeat the Gods in Heaven.) In Canton, he saw workers producing goods just like those made in America but not made for "profits for private exploiters."[28] While traveling near the Vietnam border in Kunming, Du Bois could feel up close the presence of American military advisers already in Saigon deployed to begin the long U.S. war against Vietnam to come. "It is the attempt of American business and the American Navy," he wrote, "to supplant France as colonial ruler in Southeast Asia."[29]

As we saw earlier in his "Damnation of Women" essay, Du Bois was a lifelong feminist. He was pointedly enthusiastic about the conditions of women in China. One of the slogans of the 1949 Communist revolution was "Women Hold Up Half the Sky." The slogan indicated that the revolution would try to make women equals in the proletarian revolution and to destroy old feudal sexist values. Looking at the conditions for women in China, Du Bois wrote, "They are not dressed simply for sex indulgence or beauty parades. They occupy positions from ministers of state to locomotive engineers, lawyers, doctors, clerks and laborers. They are escaping 'household drudgery.'"[30]

In a Wuhan steelworks, Du Bois marveled to his wife Shirley, "'look up there!' Alone in the engine-room sat a girl with ribboned braids, running the vast machine."[31] Du Bois concluded that compared with their counterparts in the West especially, "The women of China are becoming free."[32] Also on their visit Shirley Graham, herself a lifelong feminist, visited with Chinese women's groups and wrote about their movement towards equality, writing that they were involved at every level in trying to build a new China. After W.E.B. Du Bois's death in 1963, Shirley Graham would return to China to live, so impressed was she by the progress of the revolution. She died in Beijing a citizen of Tanzania in 1977.

Most important about his China trip for Du Bois was his renewed confidence and faith that socialism and the end of capitalism could be achieved. "China has no ranks or classes," he wrote. "Her universities grant no degrees; her government awards no medals. She has no blue book of 'society.' But she has leaders of learning and genius, scientists of renown, artisans of skill and millions who know and believe this and follow where these men lead. This is the joy of this nation, its high belief and its unfaltering hope."[33]

Du Bois made one last, brief visit to China in 1962, a year before his death. Each of these trips was criticized by the United States government as evidence that Du Bois had no loyalty to American democracy. He was as always defiant. Many African-Americans, like the NAACP organizer Robert Williams, took inspiration from Du Bois's support for the Chinese revolution. In 1963, in exile in Cuba from the United States, Williams pleaded with Mao to write a statement in support of black liberation struggle in the U.S. Mao responded by publishing his "Statement Supporting the American Negroes in Their Just Struggle Against Racial Discrimination by U.S. Imperialism."[34] The statement was released in America just weeks before Du Bois's death.

Mao's statement would inspire young black revolutionaries like Stokely Carmichael and Huey P. Newton to turn to China as an ally in the Black Power struggles in the U.S. during the 1960s. Robert Williams would follow Du Bois to Beijing, moving there in 1966 at the height of the Cultural Revolution and continuing to urge the Maoist government to support black liberation in the United States. From Beijing Williams published his newspaper *The Crusader*, full of articles praising ties between China's revolution and African-American political struggle. Other black radicals influenced by Du Bois to seek solidarity with China's Communist revolution were Vickie Garvin and members of the Marxist black nationalist group the Revolutionary Action Movement.

In his novel *Worlds of Color* (1961), one of his last written works, Du Bois made it clear how important the fight for the liberation of Asia's colonies had been in the twentieth century. His fictional protagonist Mansart opens his eyes from a nightmare and thinks:

I am back from a far journey. I saw China's millions lifting the
soil of the nation in their hands to dam the rivers which long had
eaten their land. I saw the golden domes of Moscow shining on
Russia's millions, yesterday unlettered, now reading the wisdom
of the world. I saw birds singing in Korea, Viet-Nam, Indonesia
and Malaya. I saw India and Pakistan united, free; in Paris, Ho
Chi-Minh celebrated peace on earth.[35]

We should also be critical of Du Bois's shortsighted view of China's
revolution. Du Bois either ignored or failed to report the millions of
Chinese deaths caused by the great famines during the Great Leap
Forward. Robeson Taj Frazier has aptly summarized reasons for this
absence:

The CCP's control of foreign visits and censorship of viewpoints
in opposition to the party's main line prevented many visitors
and expatriate residents from learning about . . . the GLF's
severity. Furthermore, those foreigners with knowledge of the
social upheaval's impact, particularly foreign residents of China,
added to the culture of disinformation by denying Western media
reports of famine in China. Yet it is baffling that as the Du Boises
championed the stride being made by the Chinese government,
frequently employing GLF terminology, the Chinese public at large
was beginning to contend with the real social and economic costs
of the GLF. Moreover, Chinese victims of the CCP's antirightist
campaign were simultaneously experiencing a containment
culture analoguous to, if not more severe than, that to which the
Du Boises were subjugated in the United States.[36]

Frazier here refers to China's "antirightist" campaign to arrest,
punish or expel from the Communist Party people deemed in
deviation from or opposition to the Party's ideology or political
agenda. Indeed, Du Bois painted a rosy view of proletarian life in
China in 1959 when many workers were living under strong state
repression. Du Bois's failures to report these events represents his
acceptance of China's Stalinist revolution. In much the same way his
representation of the Soviet Union on his trips there, Du Bois sought

to find only good in socialist revolutions, a sign of how far the Cold War and his own internal exile in the U.S. had shaped his political perspective.

Du Bois's support for China's Communist revolution led to his informal blacklisting during the 1950s. Most school text books that include Du Bois fail to mention it. Most of the collections of Du Bois's writings leave out his writing on Asia. But it is one of the important parts of his legacy.

When Du Bois died in 1963, Chinese magazines and newspapers mourned his death. They republished his poems and articles and recalled his support for the Chinese revolution. To this day Du Bois is revered in China as a friend of the country's struggle for national liberation, while in the U.S. his uncritical support for Mao and Maoism shadows his public reputation.

9

Final Years: Exile, Death, and Legacy

> For this is a beautiful world; this is a wonderful America, which the founding fathers dreamed until their sons drowned it in the blood of slavery and devoured it in greed. Our children must rebuild it. Let then the Dreams of the Dead rebuke the Blind who think that what is will be forever and teach them that what was worth living for must live again and that which merited death must stay dead. Teach us, forever Dead, there is no Dream but Deed, there is no Deed but memory.
>
> —W.E.B. Du Bois, *The Autobiography*

Du Bois celebrated his 90th birthday in 1958 with a party at the Roosevelt Hotel in New York. Two thousand people came and gave Du Bois a gift of $7,500. The money was important to Du Bois as his income had fallen because of the blacklist, which restricted his publishing and speaking engagements. At the birthday party, Du Bois gave a speech addressed to his great-grandson in attendance, Arthur Edward McFarlane II. In a reflective mood, Du Bois told the boy "You will fit it in the fashion in the America where eventually you will live and work to judge that life's work by the amount of money it brings you. This is a grave mistake. The return from your work must be the satisfaction which that work brings you and the world's need of that work."[1]

A little later, the great African-American artist and activist Margaret Burroughs arranged another birthday celebration in Chicago and gave him $1,700 more. Du Bois was able to use to the money to make trips to the West Indies, where he was eager to support the development of the new British West Indian Federation. The Federation formed with the intention that some Caribbean colonies, including Trinidad and Tobago, Jamaica and Barbados, might become independent of British rule as a single state.

Du Bois also spoke in 1958 at the 60th birthday party of his close friend Paul Robeson. Like Du Bois, Robeson was being blacklisted in the U.S. for his public comments defending the Soviet Union and attacking American racism and imperialism. In 1949, Robeson had been viciously attacked while singing a concert at Peekskill, New York, after saying that African-Americans would not join a war against the Soviet Union.

At Robeson's birthday party, Du Bois said "The persecution of Paul Robeson by the government and people of the United States during the last nine years has been one of the most contemptible happenings in modern history. Robeson has done nothing to hurt or defame this nation. He is, as all know, one of the most charming, charitable and loving of men."[2] Du Bois also said "In America he was a 'nigger'; in Britain he was tolerated; in France he was cheered; in the Soviet Union he was loved for the great man that he is. He loved the Soviet Union in turn."[3]

When the government finally returned his passport to him in 1958, Du Bois visited China, Eastern Europe, the Soviet Union, and Africa. He was now feeling more welcome by putatively Communist and anti-colonial states than he was in Cold War America. His message to the world was to fight for Communist revolutions and to defeat Western imperialism. He defended the Russian Revolution by writing in the Soviet journal *Literaturnaya Gazeta*, "Russians are not angels and they never were angels, they were ordinary people who were for many centuries humiliated and exploited by the same countries that now try to destroy them"—a reference to America and Russia's other capitalist enemy states.[4]

In 1958, Du Bois traveled to Tashkent, the capital of Soviet-controlled Uzbekistan, where he encouraged African countries to buy their materials from China and the Soviet Union to strengthen ties between those nations. In 1959, Du Bois was awarded the Laureate of the international Lenin Peace Prize by the Soviet Union. He continued to praise the new Soviet leader Nikhita Khrushchev, successor to Stalin, as someone who "made thousands of Americans stop looking at dark glasses and begin to learn about this great system of thought and action."[5]

Du Bois spent part of 1958 in a Soviet sanitarium near Moscow. He was suffering from exhaustion. Du Bois was in general overall good health, but the toll of the blacklist, age, and travel was beginning to show. Still, he traveled with Shirley Graham Du Bois to Sweden and then on to England, where he saw Paul Robeson in a production of *Othello*. Lawrence Bradshaw, the sculptor who created the head of Karl Marx at Highgate Cemetery, created a bust of Du Bois. Du Bois also met with several members of Parliament and the actress Katharine Hepburn in London.

Mao Tse-tung greeting W.E.B. Du Bois and Shirley Graham Du Bois, 1959. W.E.B. Du Bois Papers (MS 312). Special Collections and University Archives, University of Massachusetts Amherst Libraries

Du Bois returned briefly to the United States in 1959 before setting out again to China where, as discussed earlier, he celebrated his 91st birthday. In the same year, he published *Mansart Builds a School*, the second volume of his historical trilogy written mostly during the period of what David Levering Lewis calls his "internal

W.E.B. Du Bois shaking hands with Mao Tse-Tung, c. 1959. W.E.B. Du Bois Papers (MS 312). Special Collections and University Archives, University of Massachusetts Amherst Libraries

exile" during the 1950s blacklist period. The Mansart trilogy is a long, partly autobiographical story of Mansart, an African-American writer and intellectual who lives a life much like Du Bois's and tries to navigate the meaning of race and politics in the twentieth century. Like many books written late in his life, the Mansart triology is not studied carefully by many scholars. However, its main theme, that history can change understanding—as Du Bois puts it, "only through the present can we see the past"—helps shows how Du Bois's thinking evolved over time on questions of revolution, Communism and capitalism.

For his 92nd birthday in February 1960, Du Bois took a month-long holiday in the Virgin Islands. In June, he accepted the Lenin Peace Prize presented to him by the Soviet Union at the Soviet Embassy in

W.E.B. Du Bois accepting Lenin Peace Prize at Soviet embassy, Washington, D.C., c. June 23, 1960. W.E.B. Du Bois Papers (MS 312). Special Collections and University Archives, University of Massachusetts Amherst Libraries

Washington, D.C. The award was symbolic recognition of Du Bois's lifelong support for the Russian Revolution. On July 1, 1960, Du Bois and Shirley Graham Du Bois boarded a plane to Accra, Ghana to attend ceremonies establishing the Republic of Ghana. The event was a dream come true for Du Bois. It seemed to realize the aspiration of the Pan-African Congress formed some 60 years earlier. In Accra, Du Bois came to an agreement with independence leader and Ghanaian Prime Minister Kwame Nkrumah to form a group which could help him develop the *Encyclopedia Africana*. Since the 1930s, Du Bois had dreamed of creating a reference work detailing the history of the African world and the African diaspora.

In February 1961, Nkrumah telegraphed Du Bois, who was back in the U.S., that the Ghana Academy of Learning wished to support Du Bois's research on the *Encyclopedia*. He formally extended an invitation to come to Ghana to conduct the work. This pleased Du Bois especially because during the years of his blacklisting it had been difficult to earn support from American scholars and institutions for the *Encyclopedia* project.

Du Bois and Shirley Graham thus began making plans to move to Ghana. At about the same time, the Supreme Court of the United States upheld the constitutionality of the McCarran Internal Security Act passed in 1950. The McCarran Act was intended to force Communist organizations to register with the federal government and threatened to deport people whose writings showed sympathy for Communism. In 1953, the U.S. federal government had deported C.L.R. James for violating the McCarran Act. In 1955, the government had deported Du Bois's friend Claudia Jones for her public Communist sympathies. Both Jones and James had been arrested and imprisoned before their deportation. Both ended up living in London.

Du Bois was outraged at the Supreme Court decision. It meant that he himself might again be arrested or deported, or face trouble returning to the country if he were to travel outside its borders. On October 1, 1961, he applied for membership in the Communist Party of the United States. In his letter of application, Du Bois stated "Today, I have reached a firm conclusion. Capitalism cannot reform itself; it is doomed to self-destruction."[6] A month later, in announcing acceptance of Du Bois's application Gus Hall, the chairman of the Communist Party, praised Du Bois for joining the party at a time when the federal government was trying to "persecute Communists and suppress our party."[7]

Immediately after filing his Party membership, Du Bois and Shirley Graham left for Ghana, never to return to the U.S. They were placed in residence in an affluent section of Accra. A steady stream of international radicals and anti-colonial leaders came to visit. Du Bois hired as his assistant on the *Encyclopedia* project Alphaeus Hunton. Hunton had been a long-time member of the Communist Party of the United States before moving to Guinea to teach. Other visitors included representatives from the governments of China and Mohammed Ben Bella, leader of the Algerian National Liberation Front, then in the midst an ongoing war of decolonization against the French.

Du Bois right away set out to work on the *Encyclopedia Africana*, but because of age and health, he wrote less often and prolifically

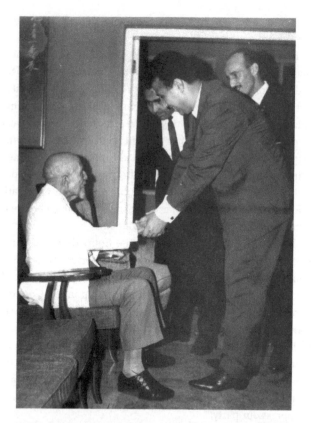

W.E.B. Du Bois greeting President Ben Bella, July 1963. W.E.B.
Du Bois Papers (MS 312). Special Collections and University
Archives, University of Massachusetts Amherst Libraries

than in previous times. A few of his last major writing projects were
revisions to his 1909 biography of John Brown, for a Soviet edition
of the book, and his *Autobiography*. The *Autobiography* was in part
an assemblage of previously published writings, but also reflections
on more than 90 years of living. Du Bois's Mansart novel *Worlds of
Color*, the last of the trilogy, was published in 1961. The book's thesis
about the present helping to explain the past referred to Du Bois
thinking about his earlier, incorrect support for imperialist Japan,
his misjudgments of the Bolshevik Revolution of 1917, and his own
anguished support for brutal aspects of Stalinism, like the violent

repressions of its peasants. At the same time, Du Bois was firm that his fundamental support for revolutions around the world had been correct, and that historical events—like Ghana's independence—was proof of that.

Meanwhile, the world around Du Bois continued to change: Algeria earned its independence from France; between 1956 and 1961, more than 20 African former colonies also gained their independence, including Nigeria, Kenya, Ivory Coast, Senegal, and Mali. Simultaneously, the U.S. began its long slow war in Vietnam; Civil Rights in the United States was propelled forward by groups like the Student Nonviolent Coordinating Committee, organized sit-ins against segregation, and an increasing awareness of the linked fates of black people in the U.S. and in Africa. By 1963, the year of Du Bois's death, African-Americans like Maya Angelou, Le Roi Jones (later Amiri Baraka) and others would all visit Kwame Nkrumah's Ghana to build solidarity at home. The slogan many of these activists eventually embraced, *Black Power*, was also the title of African-American author Richard Wright's book about Kwame Nkrumah's Convention People's Party and Ghana's fight for independence.

In one of his last published pieces, an article for the *Guardian* newspaper, Du Bois wrote of this time:

> . . . they [Negroes] are advancing rapidly today and it is clear that they have a chance to trade wide breaks in the American color line for acquiescence in American and Western European control of the world's colored peoples. This is shown by the pressure on them to keep silence on Africa and Asia and on white working class movements, and in return accept more power to vote, abolition of separation in education, dropping of "jim crow" units in our military forces and gradual disappearance of the Negro ghetto in work and housing . . . It is fair to admit that most Negroes, even those of intelligence and courage, do not fully realize that they are being bribed to trade equal status in the United States for the slavery of the majority of men.[8]

In Ghana, Du Bois continued to struggle with his health. He developed an infection to his prostate gland and underwent surgery in Rumania. But he would not go gently into the good night. "I do not apologize for living long" he wrote. "High on the ramparts of this blistering hell of life, as it must appear to most men, I sit and see the Truth."[9]

He went on:

Today the United States is the leading nation in the world, which apparently believes that war is the only way to settle present disputes and difficulties. For this reason it is spending fantastic sums of money, and wasting wealth and energy on the preparation for war, which is nothing less than criminal. Yet the United States dare not stop spending money for war. If she did her whole economy, which is today based on preparation for war, might collapse. There, we prepare for a Third World War.[10]

Du Bois's warning would later be echoed by critics of the United States war in Vietnam, like the Black Panther Party and Martin Luther King, Jr., who referred in 1967 to the "giant triplets of racism, extreme materialism, and militarism" in his call to end the war and famously called the U.S. government "the greatest purveyor of violence in the world today."[11]

As his health declined, friends from around the world expressed their concern and condolences. On his 95th birthday, February 23, 1963, Du Bois became a citizen of Ghana. His exile from the United States was now official and permanent. In the coming months, Du Bois followed preparations in Washington D.C. for the March on Washington for Jobs and Freedom organized by the Reverend Martin Luther King, Jr., and the Southern Christian Leadership Conference. The March was to protest continuing economic and political inequality for African-Americans. Du Bois had admired King from a distance and compared him to Gandhi, but the two did not have a close relationship in part because for most all of his life King disagreed with Du Bois's support for Communism.

Du Bois died in his sleep not long before King would take the stage in Washington to deliver his famous "I Have a Dream" speech. At the march in Washington, there was debate among the organizers about how to announce Du Bois's death. Du Bois's open membership

W.E.B. Du Bois on his 95th birthday with President Kwame Nkrumah and Madame Nkrumah, Accra, Ghana, February 23, 1963. W.E.B. Du Bois Papers

in the Communist Party was for many black liberals, like those who organized the march, beyond the pale.

Finally, Roy Wilkins agreed to announce Du Bois's death to the growing crowed of 250,000 people. "Regardless of the fact that in his later years Dr. Du Bois chose another path," said Wilkins, a veiled allusion to Du Bois's Communism, "it is incontrovertible that at the dawn of the twentieth century his was the voice that was calling to you to gather here today in this cause. If you want to read something that applies to 1963 go back and get a volume of *The Souls of Black Folk* by Du Bois, published in 1903."[12]

Perhaps the best epitaph for Du Bois are his own words written not longer before he died: "I believe in socialism. I seek a world where the ideals of communism will triumph—to each according to his need, from each according to his ability. For this I will work as long as I live. And I still live."[13]

Du Bois died a hero to friends and comrades on the revolutionary left, like Paul Robeson and Claudia Jones, but a pariah to mainstream

Shirley Graham Du Bois and Kwame Nkrumah beside open casket during state funeral for W.E.B. Du Bois, August 1963. W.E.B. Du Bois Papers (MS 312). Special Collections and University Archives, University of Massachusetts Amherst Libraries

America. His passing was commemorated with special journal issues in China and public fanfare in the Soviet Union, published memorials in London, and recognition across Communist bloc states like East Germany where his work was still very much alive and being read. Yet at home, many said he had gone too far in his support of Communism. *The New York Times* obituary for Du Bois underscored that he was a "monumental, but often controversial leader of Negro thought."[14] For many readers of *The Times* Du Bois had become, as the supporters of anti-Communists like Joseph McCarthy put it, "un-American."

For those on the revolutionary left today, the main contradiction of Du Bois's legacy is the tension in his thought and political action between support for what Hal Draper once called "socialism from below," that is support for the idea of working-class self-emancipation, and Stalinism, the corruption of that idea by what we have earlier diagnosed as state-capitalism and the repression of workers' efforts to control their own society. At his best moments, fueled by his understanding of the history of slavery, of the tradition of slave rebellions, and the conditions of the oppressed everywhere in the world, Du Bois's revolutionary socialism was squarely on the side of working-class self-emancipation. In a late essay published in 1956 entitled "If Eugene Debs Returned," a tribute to the militant American railroad worker, union organizer and Socialist, Du Bois aligned himself firmly with that tradition:

> Socialism includes planned production and distribution of wealth. But a completely socialistic result depends on who does the planning and for what ends. A state socialism planned by the rich for their own survival is quite possible, but it is far from the state where the rule rests in the hands of those who produce wealth and services and whose aim is the welfare of the mass of the people.[15]

At the same time, Du Bois's support for Stalin can be interpreted as a legacy of his own lifelong elitist penchant for trying to find "great leaders" to bring solutions to problems faced by the oppressed and working classes. William Gorman captured this dilemma succinctly in a 1950 assessment of where Du Bois then stood:

> For the time being his (Du Bois's) hostility to American imperialism for its long betrayal of the Negroes finds a congenial refuge in Stalinism. There he can find embodied in a single movement the two ideals which have dominated his life work in regard to the Negroes: the conception of the Talented Tenth and the urge toward international revolt. Stalinism operates on a world scale. And it approaches and manipulates the masses like an elite convinced of their backwardness and incapacity; hence the necessity to dictate, plan and administer for them from the heights of superior knowledge and wisdom.[16]

Applying Gorman's analysis to this study, we can see this contradiction played out in Du Bois's work in the difference between a work like *Black Reconstruction*, an endorsement of the struggle or "general strike" by ordinary workers, black and white, for freedom, and Du Bois's later descriptions of Franklin Roosevelt's New Deal as "socialism pure and simple." It is simply wrong to equate a federal government program of a capitalist state with "socialism" or workers' control of society.

To fully understand Du Bois's conflicts it is worth remembering not just his early dedication to the "Talented Tenth" idea for African-American racial uplift, but his early investment in reformist social democracy and even "democracy" itself. It took Du Bois many years, and much experience, to be won away from an idealist faith in bourgeois democracy and its institutions, as manifest by his one-time support for Woodrow Wilson. For a good part of his life, Du Bois thought he could work change from within the capitalism system, and that the tools of bourgeois democracy, like the vote, could be used to improve the lives of ordinary people. As he admitted at several stages, his understanding of human progress was shaped not just by slavery but by bourgeois revolutions in America and France. Only later did he realize that only ordinary working people could truly change the social relationships of their world. Indeed, Du Bois was already 49 years old, a full-grown thinker and intellectual, at the time of the Russian Revolution, long shaped and formed by the American context, and long-deprived a real education in the principles of Marxism and socialism. Delaying his understanding too was the fact that by the time Du Bois visited the Soviet Union for the first time in 1926, and began his self-education in Marxist principles, Stalinism was already in power, lending further confusion of understanding to what "real" socialism might look like in America or elsewhere. Ultimately, Du Bois's own achievements and identity as a leader of racial uplift and reform, his status as a pioneering African-American, and his hopes for his fellow African-Americans whom he dearly loved and wished to be free, produced at times an idealistic political "double consciousness" about American democracy and its potential that he expressed in his final *Autobiography*:

> I know the United States. It is my country and the land of my fathers. It is still a land of magnificent possibilities. It is still the home of noble souls and generous people. But it is selling its

birthright. It is betraying its mighty destiny. I was born on its soil and educated in its schools. I have served my country to the best of my ability. I have never knowingly broken its laws or unjustly attacked its reputation. At the same time I have pointed out its injustices and crimes and blamed it, rightly as I believe, for its mistakes. It has given me education and some of its honors, for which I am thankful.[17]

Ironically, Du Bois, who began his life seeing its promise as the promise of a nation—akin to the dreams of the "founding fathers," ended as one of that nation's harshest critics. The "double consciousness" of being "an American, a Negro" in 1903, was by the end of his life a condition of exile from the nation and its idealization. This, despite the fact that throughout his life, to the end, he longed for a place within the nation from which to dissent.

Still, upon his death, it was the dissident and pro-Communist Du Bois who was stridently emphasized in America. In 1967, four years after Du Bois's death, Martin Luther King, Jr., himself called a Communist by the FBI even though he was not one, tried to redeem Du Bois's reputation by telling Americans it was "time to cease muting the fact that Dr. Du Bois was a genius and chose to be a Communist." One year later King would himself be assassinated by a right-wing racist.

Because of his commitment to Communism, many of Du Bois's books were removed from bookshelves in the U.S. during the 1950s and even after his death. His *Autobiography*, completed just before he died, was not published in the United States until 1968, several years after it was first published in the Soviet Union.

During the Vietnam War, a group of activists including the actor Sidney Poitier, tried to raise funds to make Du Bois's childhood home in Great Barrington, Massachusetts into an historical site and to commemorate his legacy with other tributes. They were met by protests for military veterans who said Du Bois was a Communist and deserved no public tribute.[18] When the University of Massachusetts decided to name its library after Du Bois protestors argued against it for the same reason (eventually the Library did carry Du Bois's name).

His 1950 manuscript "Russia and America" remains unpublished despite efforts by scholars to bring the book into print.

But Du Bois's legacy as a revolutionary lives on in many ways around the world. In Accra, Ghana, the W.E.B. Memorial Centre for Pan-African Culture was established by Shirley Graham and W.E.B. Du Bois's son David Graham Du Bois. It remains open to students and scholars to view some of Du Bois's writings and personal effects.

Harvard University is host to the W.E.B. Du Bois Research Institute, one of the premier research centers on the history and culture of African-Americans.

In 1993, 30 years after Du Bois's death, scholar David Levering Lewis published the first of a massive two-volume biography of W.E.B. Du Bois.

After his death, Du Bois's literary executor and political mentor Herbert Aptheker, himself a member of the Communist Party, edited and published many volumes of Du Bois's writings including his newspaper columns and personal letters.

In 2007, Oxford University Press published 21 separate volumes of Du Bois's work.

Yet to this day, school children and others may know Du Bois by name, but don't know about his socialist commitments. Many readers are familiar with his early classic works like *Souls of Black Folk*, but few read his writings on China and the Soviet Union or his radical *Autobiography*. Not enough read his most important masterpiece, *Black Reconstruction*.

This is a pity and a political tragedy. Failure to contend with the full legacy of Du Bois, including his contradictory and at times wrongheaded views of socialism, has diminished understanding not just of his work but of the meaning of the socialist tradition in the United States and around the world. Honest and full accounts for example of Du Bois's life and work, as this book has aspired to be, can help students of radical ideas understand for example how Stalinism itself is a corruption of Marxist thought, and how world-historical figures like Du Bois were disserved by it. Such analysis can in turn help us understand and appreciate more fully the best of Du Bois's thought, like his work on slavery and the Civil War.

Likewise, Du Bois's support for India's decolonization and the emancipation of its working class also deserves special attention again as the current Indian state under the leadership of Narendra Modi celebrates "shining India" as an example of neoliberal capitalist success while inequality in India remains obscene. Were he alive today, Du Bois would be appalled by the income inequality sweeping across neoliberal states in Asia.

Du Bois's long-time support for the liberation of African countries should also remind us that the Arab Spring of 2011 and 2012 and its attempts to topple dictators in Egypt and Tunisia is part of a longer struggle against the legacy of colonialism.

Du Bois's support for women's rights, his opposition to atomic weapons, and his raging critique of wealth in America all remind us of movements for social justice such as Occupy, where Du Bois's criticisms of capitalism would have been right at home.

And as Americans continue to protest at dozens of police shootings and murders of black citizens, Du Bois's lifetime commitment to building a state without racism and violence should ring in our ears. There is a direct line to be drawn between Du Bois's protests of police "genocide" years ago and the Black Lives Matter movement today.

Indeed, we should remember Du Bois's cautionary parable in his book *Black Reconstruction*. Inspired by the dream and the promise of emancipation from slavery, Du Bois wrote, African-Americans "for a brief moment in the sun" began their climb to freedom, only to be pushed back by the forces of capitalism and racism towards slavery.

This titanic historical struggle for full black emancipation, for the emancipation of the working-class, is with us still.

It remains then the work of this generation and the next to understand and represent in its complete detail the revolutionary life of W.E.B. Du Bois.

Notes

Introduction: Revolutionary Lives Matter—Reclaiming W.E.B. Du Bois for Our Time

1. Civil Rights Congress, *We Charge Genocide: The Historic Petition to the United Nations for Relief From a Crime of The United States Government Against the Negro People* (New York: Civil Rights Congress, 1951) www. blackpast.org/we-charge-genocide-historic-petition-united-nations-relief-crime-united-states-government-against Accessed November 23, 2015.
2. Ibid.
3. "At the United Nations, Chicago Activists Protest Police Brutality." *The Atlantic* www.theatlantic.com/national/archive/2014/11/we-charge-genocide-movement-chicago-un/382843/ Accessed November 23, 2015.
4. W.E.B. Du Bois, "Let us Reason Together," *The Crisis* 18 (September 1919), 232.
5. W.E.B. Du Bois, "Russia, 1926," *The Crisis* 33 (November 1926), 8, in *Selections from The Crisis*, Vol. 2 (New York: Kraus International Publishers, 1983), 452.
6. W.E.B. Du Bois, "The Freeing of India" in Bill V. Mullen and Cathryn Watson, Editors. *W.E.B. Du Bois on Asia: Crossing the World Color Line* (Jackson: University Press of Mississippi, 2005) 145.
7. Walter Benjamin was one of the greatest Marxist philosophers of the twentieth century. His most famous essay on history and revolution is known as "On the Concept of History" or "Theses on the Philosophy of History." See www.marxists.org/reference/archive/benjamin/1940/history.htm Accessed November 21, 2015.
8. W.E.B. Du Bois, *The Autobiography of W.E.B. Du Bois: A Soliloquy on Viewing My Life from the Last Decade of Its First Century* (New York: International Publishers, 1968), 422.
9. David Levering Lewis, *W.E.B. Du Bois: Biography of a Race* (New York: Henry Holt and Company, 1993), 178.

Chapter 1: Childhood, Youth, and Education in an Age of Reform

1. W.E.B. Du Bois, *The Autobiography of W.E.B. Du Bois: A Soliloquy on Viewing My Life from the Last Decade of its First Century* (New York: International Publishers, 1968), 61.
2. W.E.B. Du Bois, from *Darkwater: Voices Within the Veil in W.E.B. Du Bois: A Reader*, ed. David Levering Lewis (New York: Henry Holt and Company, 1995), 116.
3. Ibid., 65.
4. Ibid., 72.
5. Ibid., 72.
6. Ibid., 72.
7. Ibid., 73.
8. Ibid., 73.
9. Ibid., 116.
10. Ibid., 115.
11. Ibid., 117.
12. Ibid., 118.
13. Ibid., 118.
14. W.E.B. Du Bois, from *The Souls of Black Folk* in *The Oxford W.E.B. Du Bois Reader*, ed. Eric J. Sundquist (Oxford: Oxford University Press, 1996), 101–102.
15. Du Bois, *Darkwater*, 118.
16. Ibid., 75.
17. W.E.B. Du Bois, *Newspaper Columns. Volume 1: 1883–1944*, ed. Herbert Aptheker (New York: Kraus International Publishers, 1986), 1.
18. Du Bois, *Newspaper Columns. V. 1*, 21.
19. Du Bois, *Autobiography*, 76.
20. Du Bois, *Darkwater*, 120.
21. Du Bois, *Autobiography*, 108.
22. Eric Porter, *The Problem of the Future World: W.E.B. Du Bois and the Race Concept at Midcentury* (Durham, NC: Duke University Press, 2010), 165.
23. Du Bois, *Autobiography*, 126.
24. Ibid., 126.
25. Ibid., 126.
26. Ibid., 132.
27. Ibid., 133.
28. Ibid., 133.

29. The German philosopher's Georg Wilhelm Friedrich Hegel's theory of the dialectic argued that change happened through oppositions resolving into a higher form. Marx adapted his theory of dialectical materialism— the class struggle between proletarian and bourgeoisie—from Hegel's dialectic. Du Bois's idea of "double consciousness" has been attributed to the influence of Hegel on his thinking.

30. W.E.B. Du Bois, "Jefferson Davis as a Representative of Civilization" in *The Oxford W.E.B. Du Bois Reader*, ed. Eric J. Sundquist (Oxford: Oxford University Press, 1996), 243.

31. David Levering Lewis, *W.E.B. Du Bois: Biography of a Race* (New York: Henry Holt and Company, 1993), 159.

32. Du Bois, *Autobiography*, 154.

33. Ibid., 245.

34. Ibid., 157.

35. Aldon Morris, *The Scholar Denied: W.E.B. Du Bois and the Birth of Modern Sociology* (Berkeley: University of California Press, 2015), 151.

36. Ibid., 151.

37. Levering Lewis, *Biography of a Race*, 144.

38. Du Bois, *Autobiography*, 168.

39. Levering Lewis, *Biography of a Race*, 144.

40. Du Bois, *Autobiography*, 162.

41. Levering Lewis, *Biography of a Race*, 149.

Chapter 2: Becoming a Scholar and Activist

1. W.E.B. Du Bois, *The Autobiography of W.E.B. Du Bois: A Soliloquy on Viewing My Life from the Last Decade of its First Century* (New York: International Publishers, 1968), 184.

2. Ibid., 184.

3. Ibid., 185.

4. Ibid., 194.

5. Ibid., 197.

6. Aldon Morris, *The Scholar Denied: W.E.B. Du Bois and the Birth of Modern Sociology* (Berkeley: University of California Press, 2015), 47.

7. Quoted in David Levering Lewis, *W.E.B. Du Bois: Biography of a Race, 1868–1919* (New York: Henry Holt, 1993), 288.

8. W.E.B. Du Bois, "The Conservation of Races" in Eric J. Sundquist, ed., *The Oxford W.E.B. Du Bois Reader* (Oxford: Oxford University Press, 1996), 40.

9. Ibid., 44.

10. See Kevin Gaines, *Uplifting the Race: Black Leaderships, Politics, and Race in the 20th Century* (Durham: University of North Carolina Press, 1996).

11. W.E.B. Du Bois, *The Philadelphia Negro: A Social Study* (Philadelphia: University of Pennsylvania Press, 1995), 5.

12. Du Bois, *The Philadelphia Negro*, 4.

13. Ibid., 199.

14. Ibid., 235.

15. Ibid., 67.

16. Ibid., 392.

17. Ibid., 285.

18. Ibid., 396.

19. Levering Lewis, *Biography of a Race*, 250.

20. Ibid., 248.

21. W.E.B. Du Bois, "To the Nations of the World" in Eric J. Sundquist, ed. *The Oxford W.E.B. Du Bois Reader* (Oxford: Oxford University Press, 1996), 625–26.

22. Ibid., 627.

23. Du Bois, *Autobiography*, 213.

24. W.E.B. Du Bois, "The Souls of Black Folk" in Eric J. Sundquist, ed. *The Oxford W.E.B. Du Bois Reader* (Oxford: Oxford University Press, 1996), 162.

25. Ibid., 106.

26. Ibid., 131.

27. Ibid., 142.

28. Ibid., 144.

29. Ibid., 180.

30. Ibid., 209.

31. Ibid., 231.

32. Levering Lewis, *Biography of a Race*, 282.

Chapter 3: Socialism, Activism, and World War I

1. W.E.B. Du Bois, "The Color Lines Belts the World" in Bill V. Mullen and Cathryn Watson, eds., *W.E.B. Du Bois on Asia: Crossing the World Color Line* (Jackson: University Press of Mississippi, 2005), 34.

2. David Levering Lewis, *W.E.B. Du Bois: Biography of a Race, 1868–1919* (New York: Henry Holt and Company, 1993), 309.

3. "The Niagara Movement: An Address to the Country" in *W.E.B. Du Bois: A Reader*, ed. David Levering Lewis (New York: Henry Holt and Company, 1995), 367.

4. Ibid., 367.

5. W.E.B. Du Bois, *The Autobiography of W.E.B. Du Bois: A Soliloquy on Viewing My Life from the Last Decade of its First Century* (New York: International Publishers, 1968), 249.

6. Du Bois, "The Niagara Movement," 369.

7. Ibid., 369; W.E.B. Du Bois, *John Brown* (New York: International Publishers, 1996), 15.

8. W.E.B. Du Bois, *Dusk of Dawn: An Essay Toward an Autobiography of a Race Concept* (New York: Schocken Books, 1968), 67.

9. Du Bois, *Autobiography*, 253.

10. Levering Lewis, *Biography of a Race*, 387.

11. Du Bois, *Autobiography*, 260.

12. Ibid., 260.

13. W.E.B. Du Bois, "The Negro and Socialism" in *Writings by W.E.B. Du Bois in Periodicals Edited by Others, Volume 1: 1891–1909*, ed. Herbert Aptheker (Millwood, NY: Kraus-Thompson, 1982), 6.

14. Ibid., 6.

15. W.E.B. Du Bois Papers on Microfilm, UMI, reel 1, frame 1119, W.E.B. Bois Papers, University of Massachusetts Amherst.

16. Ibid.

17. Mark Van Wienan, *American Socialist Triptych: The Literary-Political Work of Charlotte Perkins-Gilman, Upton Sinclair and W.E.B. Du Bois* (Ann Arbor: University of Michigan Press, 2011), 244.

18. William P. Jones, "Something to Offer." *Jacobin*, August 11, 2015 (www.jacobinmag.com/2015/08/debs-socialism-race-du-bois-socialist-party-black-liberation/) Accessed November 15, 2015.

19. Levering Lewis, *Biography of a Race*, 441.

20. Du Bios, *Autobiography*, 263.

21. W.E.B. Du Bois, "The African Roots of the War" in David Levering Lewis, ed. *W.E.B. Du Bois: A Reader* (New York: Henry Holt and Company, 1995), 642.

22. Ibid., 643.

23. Ibid., 643.

24. Ibid., 645.

25. Ibid., 643.

26. Ibid., 647.

27. Ibid., 647.

28. Ibid., 647.

29. See Vladimir Lenin, "Imperialism is the Highest Stage of Capitalism" (www.marxists.org/archive/lenin/works/1916/imp-hsc/) Accessed November 24, 2015.

30. Du Bois, "African Roots of the War," 650.

31. Du Bois, *Autobiography*, 274.

32. Levering Lewis, *Biography of a Race*, 526.

33. Du Bois, *Autobiography*, 271.

34. W.E.B. Du Bois, from *Darkwater: Voices From Within the Veil*, in *The Oxford W.E.B. Du Bois Reader*, ed. Eric J. Sundquist (Oxford: Oxford University Press, 1996), 485.

35. Ibid., 516.

36. Ibid., 531.

37. Ibid., 534.

38. W.E.B. Du Bois, "The Damnation of Women" in *The Oxford W.E.B. Du Bois Reader*, ed. Eric J. Sundquist (Oxford: Oxford University Press, 1996), 565.

39. Ibid., 565.

40. Ibid., 567.

41. Ibid., 569.

42. Ibid., 569.

43. Ibid., 573.

44. Ibid., 574.

45. Du Bois, *Autobiography*, 232.

Chapter 4: Du Bois and the Russian Revolution

1. W.E.B. Du Bois, *Dusk of Dawn: An Essay Toward an Autobiography of a Race Concept* (New York: Schocken Books, 1968), 285.

2. See Gerald Horne, *Black and Red: W.E.B. Du Bois and the Afro-American Response to the Cold War* (Albany: SUNY Press, 1986); Manning Marable, *W.E.B. Du Bois: Black Radical Democrat* (New York: Routledge, 1986); Cedric Robinson, *Black Marxism: The Making of the Black Radical Tradition* (Chapel Hill: University of North Carolina Press, 1983).

3. Quoted in Lars Lih, *Lenin* (London: Reaktion Books, 2011), 96.

4. W.E.B. Du Bois, "Russia and America: An Interpretation," unpublished draft manuscript 1950. Microfilm W.E.B. Du Bois Papers, University of Massachusetts, Amherst, 23.

5. W.E.B. Du Bois, "Worlds of Color," *Foreign Affairs*, N. 18 (April 1925), 442.

6. W.E.B. Du Bois, *In Battle for Peace* (New York: Masses & Mainstream, 1952), 117.

7. W.E.B. Du Bois, "Russia and America," 10.

8. W.E.B. Du Bois, "Let us Reason Together," *The Crisis* 18 (September 1919), 234–35.

9. David Levering Lewis, *W.E.B. Du Bois: Biography of a Race* (New York: Henry Holt, 1993), 531.

10. Claude McKay, 'Soviet Russia and the Negro," *The Crisis* 27 (December 1923): 61–65.

11. W.E.B. Du Bois, "Opinion," *The Crisis* 22, no. 3 (July 1921): 114.

12. Vladimir Ilych Lenin, "The Right of Nations to Self-Determination," available at www.marxists.org/archive/lenin/works/1914/self-det/ (accessed November 24, 2015).

13. W.E.B. Du Bois et al., "Manifesto of the Second Pan-African Congress" in Eric J. Sundquist, ed. *The Oxford W.E.B. Du Bois Reader* (Oxford: Oxford University Press, 1996), 644.

14. See Karuna Kaushik, *Russian Revolution and Indian Nationalism: Studies of Lajpat Rai, Suhas Chandra Bose and Rammanohar Lohia* (New Delhi: Chanayaka, 1984), 45–46.

15. Dohra Ahmad, *Landscapes of Hope: Anti-Colonial Utopianism in America* (Oxford: Oxford University Press, 2009), 172.

16. Levering Lewis, *Biography of a Race*, 196.

17. Du Bois, "Russia and America," 19.

18. Levering Lewis, *Biography of a Race*, 202. See also Duncan Hallas, *The Comintern* (Chicago: Haymarket Books, 2007), 29.

19. Du Bois, "Russia and America," 18.

20. Ibid., 27.

21. Ibid., 25.

22. W.E.B. Du Bois, *Dark Princess: A Romance* (Jackson: University Press of Mississippi, 1995), 226.

23. Ibid., 270.

24. Mark Van Wienan, *American Socialist Triptych: The Literary-Poiltical Work of Charlotte Perkins Gilman, Upton Sinclair and W.E.B. Du Bois* (Ann Arbor: University of Michigan Press, 2011), 270–71.

Chapter 5: The Depression, Black Reconstruction, and Du Bois's Asia Turn

1. W.E.B. Du Bois, "Russia and America: An Interpretation," unpublished draft manuscript 1950. Microfilm W.E.B. Du Bois Papers, University of Massachusetts, Amherst, 37.

2. W.E.B. Du Bois, "Letter to Algernon Lee," February 15, 1929, in Herbert Aptheker, ed., *The Correspondence of W.E.B. Du Bois. V. 1* (Amherst: University of Massachusetts Press, 1997), 389.

3. Glenda Gilmore, *Defying Dixie: The Radical Roots of Civil Rights, 1919–1950* (New York: W.W. Norton, 2008), 99.

4. Quoted in ibid., 264–65.

5. Ibid.

6. Mark Van Wienan, *American Socialist Triptych: The Literary-Poiltical Work of Charlotte Perkins Gilman, Upton Sinclair and W.E.B. Du Bois* (Ann Arbor: University of Michigan Press, 2011), 281.

7. Ibid., 278.

8. W.E.B. Du Bois, "The Negro and Communism" in *The Oxford W.E.B. Du Bois Reader*, ed. Eric J. Sundquist (Oxford: Oxford University Press, 1996), 409.

9. W.E.B. Du Bois, "A Negro Nation Within the Nation" in Eric J. Sundquist, ed. *The Oxford W.E.B. Du Bois Reader* (Oxford: Oxford University Press, 1996), 435; italics added.

10. W.E.B. Du Bois, "Forum of Fact and Opinion" in W.E.B. Du Bois, *Newspaper Columns. Volume 1: 1883–1944*, ed. Herbert Aptheker (New York: Kraus International Publishers, 1986), 82–83, and, later, W.E.B. Du Bois, *Dusk of Dawn: An Essay Toward an Autobiography of a Race Concept* (New York: Schocken Books, 1968), 320–22.

11. W.E.B. Du Bois, "Letter to George Streator" April 24, 1935, in Herbert Aptheker, ed., *The Correspondence of W.E.B. Du Bois, V. I,* 90.

12. W.E.B. Du Bois, *Black Reconstruction in America 1860–1880* (New York: Free Press, 1998), 434.

13. Marx's quote may be found in Karl Marx, *Capital,* vol. 1, chapter 10 "The Working Day," section 7 (New York: International Publishers, 1967), 301.

14. Du Bois, *Black Reconstruction in America,* 708.

15. Ibid., 15.

16. Ibid., 16.

17. Du Bois used the term "wages of whiteness" to refer to the psychological and social benefits whites had that African-Americans did not have living in a racist society. For more on this topic see Theodore Allen, *The Invention of the White Race: Racial Oppression and Social Control. V. 1* (New York: Version, 2012) and Gregory Meyerson "Rethinking Black Marxism: Reflections on Cedric Robinson and Others" in Cultural Logic http://clogic.eserver.org/3–1&2/meyerson.html (Accessed November 24, 2015).

18. W.E.B. Du Bois, "Listen Japan and China" in *W.E.B. Du Bois on Asia: Crossing the World Color Line*, eds. Bill V. Mullen and Cathryn Watson (Jackson: University Press of Mississippi, 2005), 74.

19. W.E.B. Du Bois, "What Japan Has Done" in Mullen and Watson, *W.E.B. Du Bois on Asia*, 78.

20. Ibid., 78.

21. Yuichiro Onishi, *Transpacific Antiracism: Afro-Asian Solidarity in 20th Century Black America, Japan, and Okinawa* (New York: New York University Press, 2013), 76.

22. W.E.B. Du Bois, "Man Power" in Mullen and Watson, *W.E.B. Du Bois on Asia*, 76.

23. W.E.B. Du Bois, "Forum of Fact and Opinion" in *Newspaper Columns by W.E.B. Du Bois. V. 1*, 172.

24. W.E.B. Du Bois, *The Autobiography of W.E.B. Du Bois: A Soliloquy on Viewing My Life from the Last Decade of Its First Century* (New York: International Publishers, 1968), 50.

25. Du Bois, *Worlds of Color: The Black Flame Trilogy V. 3* (Oxford: Oxford University Press, 2007), 43.

26. W.E.B. Du Bois, *Dusk of Dawn*, 321.

Chapter 6: Pan-Africanism or Communism?

1. W.E.B. Du Bois, "Africa and the Slave Trade" in *The Oxford W.E.B. Du Bois Reader*, ed. Eric J. Sundquist (Oxford: Oxford University Press, 1996), 628.

2. David Levering Lewis, *W.E.B. Du Bois: Biography of a Race* (New York: Henry Holt, 1993), 118.

3. Ibid., 118.

4. Ibid., 123.

5. Ibid., 127.

6. W.E.B. Du Bois, "Little Portraits of Africa" in *The Oxford W.E.B. Du Bois Reader*, ed. Eric J. Sundquist (Oxford: Oxford University Press, 1996), 646.

7. Quoted in James Hooker, *Black Revolutionary: George Padmore's Path from Communism to Pan-Africanism* (New York: Frederick A. Praeger, 1967), 24.

8. Ibid.

9. C.L.R. James, *A History of Pan-African Revolt* (New York: PM Press, 2012), 32.

10. W.E.B. Du Bois, "The Realities in Africa" in *The Oxford W.E.B. Du Bois Reader*, ed. Eric J. Sundquist (Oxford: Oxford University Press, 1996), 659.

11. Ibid., 660.

12. Quoted in Hakim Adi and Marika Sherwood, *The 1945 Manchester Pan-African Congress Revisited* (London: New Beacon, 1995), 18.

13. Ibid., 21.

14. David Levering Lewis, *W.E.B. Du Bois: The Fight for Equality and the American Century, 1919–1963* (New York: Henry Holt and Company, 2000), 500.

15. Adi and Sherwood, *The 1945 Manchester Pan-African Congress Revisited*, 20.

16. Ibid.

17. Paris 1945: *Report of the World Trade Union Conference Congress, September 25–October 8, 1945*, World Trade Union Congress, 1945, 1.

18. Ibid., 179.

19. Quoted in Hooker, *Black Revolutionary*, 95.

20. Adi and Sherwood, *The 1945 Manchester Pan-African Congress Revisited*, 80.

21. W.E.B. Du Bois, "Pan-Africanism: A Mission in My Life" in *W.E.B. Du Bois: A Reader*, ed. Andrew Paschal (New York: Macmillan, 1971), 251.

22. Quoted in Adi and Sherwood, *The 1945 Manchester Pan-African Congress Revisited*, 56.

23. Quoted in ibid., 62.

24. Julius K. Nyerere, *Freedom and Socialism/Uhuru na Ujamaa: A Selection from Writings and Speeches, 1965–1967* (Dar es Salaam, Tanzania: Oxford University Press, 1968), 15.

25. W.E.B. Du Bois, "Letter to George Padmore" in Herbert Aptheker, ed., *The Correspondence of W.E.B. Du Bois*, 3:375.

26. George Padmore, *How Russia Transformed Her Colonial Empire: A Challenge to the Imperialist Powers* (London: Dennis Dobson, 1946), xii.

27. W.E.B. Du Bois, "Africa's Choice," *National Guardian*, October 29, 1956, in *Newspaper Columns by W.E.B. Du Bois. Volume 2: Selections from 1945–1961*, ed. Herbert Aptheker (White Plains, NY: Kraus-Thomson, 1986), 973.

28. Ibid., 179.

29. Frantz Fanon, the psychiatrist and anti-colonial fighter in the war of Algerian independence, warned about corruptions of colonial struggles by ruling elites in several of his works, most especially in *The Wretched of the Earth* (New York: Grove Press, 1963).

30. W.E.B. Du Bois, *The Autobiography of W.E.B. Du Bois: A Soliloquy on Viewing My Life from the Last Decade of Its First Century* (New York: International Publishers, 1968), 400.

31. Ibid., 404.

32. W.E.B. Du Bois, "American Negroes and Africa's Rise to Freedom" in Paschal, *A W.E.B. Du Bois Reader*, 15.

33. W.E.B. Du Bois, "Watch Africa" in Aptheker, *Newspaper Columns by W.E.B. Du Bois. V. 2*, 863.

Chapter 7: Wrestling with the Cold War, Stalinism, and the Blacklist

1. David Levering Lewis, *W.E.B. Du Bois: Biography of a Race* (New York: Henry Holt, 1993), 524.

2. Ibid., 525.

3. See William Maxwell, *F.B. Eyes: How J. Edgar Hoover's Ghostreaders Framed African-American Literature* (Princeton: Princeton University Press, 2015).

4. Marable, Manning, *Race, Reform, and Rebellion: The Second Black Reconstruction in America, 1945–1982* (Jackson: University Press of Mississippi, 1984), 33.

5. W.E.B. Du Bois, *The Autobiography of W.E.B. Du Bois: A Soliloquy on Viewing My Life from the Last Decade of Its First Century* (New York: International Publishers, 1968), 354.

6. Ibid., 355.

7. Ibid., 355.

8. Quoted in Marali Balaji, *The Professor and the Pupil: The Politics and Friendship of W.E.B. Du Bois and Paul Robeson* (New York: Nation Books, 207), 300.

9. W.E.B. Du Bois, "On the Future of the American Negro," *Freedomways* 5, no. 1 (Winter 1965): 124.

10. Quoted in Gerald Horne, *Race Woman: The Lives of Shirley Graham Du Bois* (New York: New York University Press, 2002), 122–23.

11. The only biography of Shirley Graham Du Bois is Horne's *Race Woman*.

12. In addition to Horne, for more information on David Graham Du Bois see Alex Lubin, *Geographies of Liberation: The Making of an Afro-Arab Political Imaginary* (Chapel Hill: University of North Carolina Press, 2014).

13. Du Bois, *Autobiography*, 358.

14. Ibid., 359.

15. Ibid., 363.

16. Ibid., 376. See also "Watchword for Negroes: Register and Vote!" in Julius Lester, ed., *The Seventh Son: The Thought and Writings of W.E.B. Du Bois,* Volume 2 (New York: Vintage Books, 1971), pp. 652–53.

17. Ibid., 377.

18. Ibid., 377.

19. Ibid., 388.

20. Ibid., 391.

21. Ibid., 395.

22. Ibid., 396.

23. W.E.B. Du Bois, "Russia and America: An Interpretation," unpublished draft manuscript 1950. Microfilm W.E.B. Du Bois Papers, University of Massachusetts, Amherst.

24. Ibid., 77–78.

25. Ibid., 77.

26. W.E.B. Du Bois, "Joseph Stalin" in *The Oxford W.E.B. Du Bois Reader,* ed. Eric J. Sundquist (Oxford: Oxford University Press, 1996), 287.

27. Ibid., 288.

28. Ibid.

29. Ibid., 289.

30. See *Marcel van der Linden, Western Marxism and the Soviet Union: A Survey of Critical Theories and Debates Since 1917* (Chicago: Haymarket Books, 2009), pp. 49–68, 107–26, 180–93, 258–80. For a particularly cogent development of this analysis, see Tony Cliff, *State Capitalism in Russia* (London: Pluto Press, 1974).

31. W.E.B. Du Bois, "World Changer," review of Anna Louise Strong, *The Stalin Era* in *Masses & Mainstream,* January 1957, 5.

32. W.E.B. Du Bois, "Nevidannyi Skachok" [An Unprecedented Leap], *Literaturnaya Gazeta,* November 5, 1957, 5.

33. "If Eugene Debs Returned" in Philip S. Foner, ed., *W.E.B. Du Bois Speaks, Speeches and Addresses 1920–1963* (New York: Pathfinder Press, 1970), pp. 286, 287; "The Independentocrat at the Dinner Table" in Julius Lester, ed., *The Seventh Son: The Thought and Writings of W.E.B. Du Bois,* Volume 2 (New York: Vintage Books, 1971), pp. 654–56.

Chapter 8: The East is Red: Supporting Revolutions in Asia

1. W.E.B. Du Bois, "Forum of Fact and Opinion" in *Newspaper Columns by W.E.B. Du Bois, Volume 1: Selections from 1883–1944,* ed. Herbert Aptheker (White Plains, NY: Kraus-Thomson, 1986), 174.

2. W.E.B. Du Bois, "Prospect of a World Without Racial Conflict" in *W.E.B. Du Bois on Asia: Crossing the World Color Line*, ed. Bill V. Mullen and Cathryn Watson (Jackson: University Press of Mississippi, 2005), 130.

3. W.E.B. Du Bois, "Asia in Africa" in Mullen and Watson, *W.E.B. Du Bois on Asia*, 13.

4. Robeson Taj Frazier, *The East is Black: Cold War China in the Black Radical Imagination* (Durham: Duke University Press, 2015), 45.

5. Ibid., 45.

6. W.E.B. Du Bois, "The Winds of Time" in *Newspaper Columns of W.E.B. Du Bois, Volume 2: Selections from 1945–1961*, ed. Herbert Aptheker (White Plains, NY: Kraus-Thomson, 1986), 754.

7. W.E.B. Du Bois, "Africa Today" in Aptheker, *Newspapers Columns of W.E.B. Du Bois, V. 2*, 855.

8. W.E.B. Du Bois, "The Freeing of India" in Mullen and Watson, *W.E.B. Du Bois on Asia*, 145.

9. W.E.B. Du Bois, "Letter to Jawaharlal Nehru," December 26, 1956, W.E.B. Du Bois Papers, University of Massachusetts Amherst, reel 72, no. 1.

10. W.E.B. Du Bois, "The Freeing of India" in Mullen and Watson, *W.E.B. Du Bois on Asia*, 153.

11. W.E.B. Du Bois, "Gandhi and the American Negroes" in *The Oxford W.E.B. Du Bois Reader*, ed. Eric J. Sundquist (Oxford: Oxford University Press, 1996), 296.

12. W.E.B. Du Bois, "Will the Great Gandhi Live Again?" in Mullen and Watson, *W.E.B. Du Bois on Asia*, 185.

13. W.E.B. Du Bois, *The Autobiography of W.E.B. Du Bois: A Soliloquy on Viewing My Life from the Last Decade of Its First Century* (New York: International Publishers, 1968), 349.

14. Ibid., 350.

15. Ibid., 358.

16. W.E.B. Du Bois, "Indonesia" in Mullen and Watson, *W.E.B. Du Bois on Asia*, 177.

17. W.E.B. Du Bois, "Prospect of a World Without Racial Conflict" in Mullen and Watson, *W.E.B. Du Bois on Asia*, 128.

18. Ibid.

19. Robin D.G. Kelley, "Israel's Black Apologists" in *Apartheid Israel: The Politics of an Analogy*, ed. Jon Soske and Sean Jacobs (Chicago: Haymarket Books, 2015), 132.

20. Frazier, *East is Black*, 45.

21. W.E.B. Du Bois, "Our Visit to China" in ed. Mullen and Watson, *W.E.B. Du Bois on Asia*, 189.

22. Du Bois, *Autobiography*, 47.

23. Ibid., 49.

24. David Levering Lewis, *W.E.B. Du Bois: Biography of a Race* (New York: Henry Holt, 1993), 564.

25. Du Bois, *Autobiography*, 187.

26. Levering Lewis, *Biography of a Race*, 564.

27. Ibid.

28. Du Bois, *Autobiography*, 49.

29. Ibid.

30. Ibid., 48.

31. Ibid., 52.

32. Ibid., 52–53.

33. Ibid., 52.

34. Mao Tse-Tung, "Statement Supporting the Negro People in Their Just Struggle Against Racial Discrimination by U.S. Imperialism, August 8, 1963" in *Afro-Asia: Revolutionary Political and Cultural Connections Between African-Americans and Asian-Americans*, ed. Fred Ho and Bill V. Mullen (Durham: Duke University Press, 2008), 91–93. For more on Du Bois in China see Robeson Taj Frazier, *The East is Black: Cold War China in the Black Radical Imagination* (Durham: Duke University Press, 2015).

35. W.E.B. Du Bois, *Worlds of Color: The Black Flame Trilogy*, Volume 3 (Oxford: Oxford University Press, 2007), 288.

36. Frazier, *The East is Black*, 51.

Chapter 9: Final Years: Exile, Death and Legacy

1. W.E.B. Du Bois, *The Autobiography of W.E.B. Du Bois: A Soliloquy on Viewing My Life from the Last Decade of Its First Century* (New York: International Publishers, 1968), 398.

2. Ibid., 396.

3. Ibid., 397.

4. W.E.B. Du Bois, "Nevidannyi Skachok" [An Unprecedented Leap], *Literaturnaya Gazeta*, November 5, 1957, 5.

5. W.E.B. Du Bois, "Triumf Sotsializma" [The Triumph of Socialism], *Izvestia*, November 7, 1959, 5.

6. David Levering Lewis, *W.E.B. Du Bois: Biography of a Race* (New York: Henry Holt, 1993), 567.

7. Peter Kihss, "W.E.B. Du Bois Joins Communist Party at 93." *New York Times*. November 23, 1961. www.nytimes.com/books/00/11/05/specials/dubois-communist.html (Accessed December 5, 2015).

8. W.E.B. Du Bois, "Negroes and the Third World" in *W.E.B. Du Bois: A Reader*, ed. Andrew Paschal (New York: Macmillan, 1971), 17.

9. Du Bois, *Autobiography*, 415.

10. Ibid., 419.

11. Martin Luther King, Jr., "Beyond Vietnam" in *Voices of a People's History of the United States*, ed. Howard Zinn and Anthony Arnove (New York: Seven Stories Press, 2009), 425–26.

12. Charles Euchner, *Nobody Turn Me Around: A People's History of the March on Washington, 1963* (Boston: Beacon Press, 2010), 233.

13. W.E.B. Du Bois, *Autobiography*, 421–22.

14. "W.E.B. Du Bois Dies in Ghana; Negro Leader and Author, 95." August 28, 1963. www.nytimes.com/learning/general/onthisday/bday/0223.html. www.nytimes.com/learning/general/onthisday/bday/0223.html (Accessed December 2, 2015).

15. W.E.B. Du Bois, "If Eugene Debs Returned." *American Socialist*, November 28, 1955, 311.

16. William Gorman, "W.E.B. Du Bois and His Work." *Fourth International*, May–June 1950, V. 11, N. 3. 85.

17. Du Bois, *Autobiography*, 419.

18. Amy Bass's *Those About Him Remained Silent: The Battle Over W.E.B. Du Bois* (Minneapolis: University of Minnesota Press, 2012) is a fine account of the political fight over Du Bois's legacy.

Further Reading

Bass, Amy. *Those About Him Remained Silent: The Battle Over W.E.B. Du Bois* (Minneapolis: University of Minnesota Press, 2012). Bass describes the struggle over the commemoration of Du Bois's legacy between Black leftists and conservatives during and after the Vietnam War in his hometown of Great Barrington, Massachusetts.

Du Bois, W.E.B. *The Autobiography of W.E.B. Du Bois: A Soliloquy on Viewing My Life from the Last Decade of its First Century* (New York: International Publishers, 1968). The final summation by Du Bois of his own life written in his final years and not published until after his death.

——*Black Reconstruction in America 1860–1880* (New York: Free Press, 1998). Du Bois's magisterial history of the role of African-Americans in their emancipation from slavery during and after the U.S. Civil War.

——*In Battle for Peace* (New York: Masses & Mainstream, 1952). Du Bois's account of his indictment and trial by the U.S. federal government for his work with the Peace Information Center, a group dedicated to eliminating atomic weapons.

——*Souls of Black Folk* in *The Oxford W.E.B. Du Bois*, ed. Eric J. Sundquist (Oxford: Oxford University Press, 1996), 97–240. Du Bois's classic 1903 book which popularized his ideas about "double consciousness" for African-Americans as well as his famous declaration, "The twentieth century will be the century of the color line."

Horne, Gerald. *Black and Red: W.E.B. Du Bois and the Afro-American Response to the Cold War* (Albany: SUNY Press, 1986). An important, sympathetic account of Du Bois's turn to socialism during the Cold War and the backlash that ensued against him.

——*Race Woman: The Lives of Shirley Graham Du Bois* (New York: New York University Press, 2002). The only extant biography of Shirley Graham Du Bois, a lifelong activist and artist and Du Bois's political companion and second wife.

Lewis, David Levering. *W.E.B. Du Bois: Biography of a Race* (New York: Henry Holt and Company, 1993). Part 1 of Lewis's expansive and detailed biography of Du Bois's life.

———W.E.B. Du Bois: The Fight for Equality and the American Century, 1919–1963 (New York: Henry Holt and Company, 2000). The second part of Lewis's study.

Marable, Manning. *W.E.B. Du Bois: Black Radical Democrat* (New York: Routledge, 1986). A political biography of Du Bois as political radical by the distinguished late historian.

Morris, Aldon. *The Scholar Denied: W.E.B. Du Bois and the Birth of Modern Sociology* (Berkeley: University of California Press, 2015). A recent groundbreaking study which demonstrates how Du Bois and a circle of African-American intellectuals helped develop the field of sociology at the turn of the twentieth century.

Padmore, George. *Pan-Africanism or Communism? The Coming Struggle for Africa* (London: D. Dobson, 1961). An important book on the relationship of the Pan-African movement to socialism and Communism by Du Bois's friend and collaborator.

Van Wienan, Mark. *American Socialist Triptych: The Literary-Political Work of Charlotte Perkins-Gilman, Upton Sinclair and W.E.B. Du Bois* (Ann Arbor: University of Michigan Press, 2011). This study situates Du Bois and his political views of socialism among other early prominent socialists at the turn of the twentieth century.

Index

Acheson, Dean, 114
African Blood Brotherhood, 62
All-India Muslim League, 126
American Negro Academy, 23–4
American Negro Labor Congress, 66,
    92
Angelou, Maya, 102, 143
Aptheker, Herbert, 57, 150
Atlanta Race Riots, 41
Atlantic Charter, 94
Atlantic Monthly, 32

Babu, Abdul, 104
Bakunin, Mikhail, 19
Bandung Conference, 129–30
Baraka, Amiri (Leroi Jones), 102,
    143
Ben Bella, Mohammed, 141, 142
Benjamin, Walter, 6, 153n
Berger, Victor, 44
Berlin Conference, 18
Bernstein, Eduard, 19
Birth of a Nation, 42
Black Belt Thesis, 63
Black Lives Matter Movement, 151
Black Panther Party, 103, 144
*Black Reconstruction in America,
    1860–1880*, 4, 6, 58, 73, 78–82, 93,
    147
Bolshevik Revolution, 57, 117, 142
Bradshaw, Lawrence, 138
Briggs, Cyril, 61
Brotherhood of Sleeping Car Porters,
    75

Brown, John, 40
Burroughs, Margaret, 136

Carmichael, Stokely, 133
Cesaire, Aime, 93
Chandler, Owen, 61
Chattopadhyaya, Virendranath, 69
Chesnutt, Charles, 25
Chiang Kai-shek, 123, 125, 126
China's 1911 Revolution, 82
Chinese Revolution of 1949, 123,
    124, 129
Churchill, Winston, 107
Citron, Alice, 116
Civil Rights Congress, 1
Cleaver, Eldridge, 103
Cliff, Tony, 120
COINTELPRO, 109
Cold War, 107
Committee for a Democratic Far
    Eastern Policy, 125
Communist International
    (Comintern), 4, 49, 59–60; and
    Black Belt Thesis, 63, 71
Communist Party of the United
    States, 3, 75, 108
Cooper, Anna Julia, 29
Council of African Affairs, 109
Crisis, 4, 41, 43
Crummell, Alexander, 23; influence
    on Du Bois, 23
Cullen, Countee, 111
Cultural and Scientific Conference
    for World Peace, 127

Dark Princess: A Romance, 19, 69–71, 82

Davis, Jefferson, 17

Debs, Eugene, 44, 58, 122

Delany, Martin Robinson, 23

DePriest, Oscar, 91

Diagne, Blaise, 64

Draper, Hal, 146

Du Bois, Alfred, 9

Du Bois, Shirley Graham, 4, 93, 102, 103, 112–13, 150; marriage to W.E.B., 113; death of, 132, 138, 141, 146

Du Bois, W.E.B. and "double consciousness" idea, 16, 33; at Harvard, 18; at University of Berlin, 18; and Marxism, 19; and "The Conservation of Races" 25–6; at Atlanta University, 32; on Booker T. Washington, 34; and "Sorrow Songs," 36; criticism of Booker T. Washington, 38–40; book on John Brown, 40–1; membership in Socialist Party, 43; and socialism, 43–5, 75, 78; and "African Roots of War," 46–7; and *Darkwater: Voices From Within the Veil*, 50–3; "The Damnation of Women," 51–2; *The Quest of the Silver Fleece*, 53; "Russia and America" manuscript, 57, 86, 118–19, 150; and Russian Revolution, 60–1, 71; first visit to Soviet Union, 66–8; "The Negro and Marxism," 75; and Marxism, 74–5; and economic cooperatives, 74–5; on Japan, 83–6; on Africa, 89–90; debate with George Padmore, 99–100; *In Battle for*

Peace, 115; travel to China, 130–3; receives Lenin Peace Prize, 137, 140; *Worlds of Color*, 142; *Mansart Builds a School*, 138; move to Ghana, 144–5; and W.E.B. Memorial Centre for Pan-African Culture, 150

Dunbar, Paul Laurence, 23, 25

Dusk of Dawn, 87, 98

Egypt, 5

Emancipation Proclamation, 15

Encyclopedia Africana, 140–1

Ethiopia, 18

Fanon, Frantz, 101

Fast, Howard, 108

Fauset, Jessie Redmon, 25, 43

Fisk University, 14, 16

Fortune, Timothy Thomas, 13

Fort-Whitman, Lovett, 66

Frazier, Robeson Taj, 134

French Revolution, 119

Gandhi, Mohandas, 87, 126, 127

Gaines, Kevin, 26

Garnet, Henry Highland, 23

Garvey, Marcus, 61

Garvin, Vickie, 134

Gomer, Nina, 21, 36 (caption); death of, 111

Gorman, William, 147

Great Barrington, MA, 9

Great Depression, 72–3

Great Leap Forward (China), 123–4, 130

Haitian Revolution, 18

Hall, Gus, 141

Harrison, Hubert, 61
Haywood, Harry, 63, 66
Hegel, Georg Wilhelm Friedrich, 155n
Hiroshima bombing, 111
Holocaust, 128
Hoover, J. Edgar, 109
House Un-American Activities Committee, 109
Hughes, Langston, 67
Hunton, Alphaeus, 141

India, 5
Indonesian Republic, 128
Intercollegiate Socialist Society, 49
International African Service Bureau, 93
International Labor Defense, 75
International Labor Organization, 94
Israel, 128, 129

James, C.L.R., 4, 80; *The Black Jacobins*, 80, 92; *A History of Pan-African Revolt*, 81, 82, 93; *World Revolution 1917–1936: The Rise and Fall of the Communist International*, 92, 120, 141
James, William, 16
Japan and Japanese Imperialism, 83–6
Jim Crow, 21
Jinnah, Muhammad Ali, 126
Johnson, James Weldon, 74
Johnson, Manning, 110
Jones, Claudia, 53, 93, 113, 141, 145
Junior NAACP, 43

Kagawa, Toyohiko, 83
Kelley, Florence, 42

Kelley, Robin D.G., 129
Kenyatta, Jomo, 93, 96
Khrushchev, Nikita, 121, 137
King, Jr., Martin Luther, 3, 143, 149
Kuomintang (Nationalist Party China), 125

Lajpat Rai, Lala, 65–6; influence on Du Bois, 66
League of Nations, 65
Lee, Algernon, 74
Lenin, Vladimir Ilyich, 4, 38; *Imperialism: The Highest Stage of Capitalism*, 48, 58, 60; "The Right to Self-Determination," 64
Lewis, David Levering, 6, 37, 138, 150
Lincoln, Abraham, 78
Locke, Alain, 61
L'Ouverture, Toussaint, 18
Luce, Henry, 123

Madame Chiang Kai-shek, 125
Marable, Manning, 57
Marcontonio, Vito, 115
Martin, Trayvon, 2
Marx, Karl, 58, 80; *The Civil War in France*, 80
Masses & Mainstream, 113
Mazri, Ali, 104
McCarran Internal Security Act, 141
McCarthy, Joseph, 146
McCarthyism, 3
McKay, Claude, 62; and *Negri v. Ameriki (The Negro in America)*, 63, 66, 67, 82
The Messenger, 61
Miller, Kelly, 23
Milliard, Peter, 96
Modi, Narendra, 151

Morris, Aldon, 19, 23, 32

Nagasaki bombing, 111
National Afro-American League, 13
National Association for the
    Advancement of Colored People
    (NAACP), 4, 25, 41, 75, 97, 109
National Guardian, 104, 115, 122
The Negro (Du Bois book), 89, 102
Negro Suffrage League, 39
Nehru, Jawarhalal, 4, 102, 126, 127
New York *Globe*, 13
Newton, Huey, 103, 134
Niagara Movement, 38, 40
New York Times, 146
Nkrumah, Francis, 95
Nkrumah, Kwame, 93, 96, 98, 99,
    102, 103, 121, 140, 143, 145, 146
Nyerere, Julius, 99, 103; *Ujaamma*,
    104

Ovington, Mary White, 42

Padmore, George, 4, 82, 87, 90–2;
    and Black Belt Thesis, 90; *The Life
    and Struggle of Negro Toilers*, 91,
    93; *Pan-Africanism or Communism?
    The Coming Struggle for Africa*, 91,
    100; *Africa and World Peace*, 93;
    *Colonial and Coloured Unity: A
    Program for Action*, 98; *How Russia
    Transformed Her Colonial Empire:
    A Challenge to the Imperialist
    Powers*, 99
Pan-African Congress 1900, 29–32
Pan-African Congress 1919, 32, 49,
    64
Pan-African Congress 1923, 65
Pan-African Congress 1927, 90

Pan-African Congress 1945, 96–8
Pan-African Federation, 94, 95, 96
Paris Commune, 81
Patterson, Louise, 53
Peace Information Center, 3, 114, 115
Philadelphia Negro (Du Bois), 27–9,
    59
Phillips, Wendell, 14
Pittsburgh Courier, 77
Plessy versus Ferguson, 27
Porter, Eric, 16, 33

Randolph, A. Phillip, 61, 70, 75, 82
Red International of Labor Unions,
    91
"Red Summer," 60, 62
Ricardo, David, 16
Robeson, Paul, 57, 67, 108, 109, 110,
    113, 121, 137, 138, 145
Robinson, Cedric, 57, 79
Roosevelt, Franklin, 118
Roosevelt, Theodore, 38
Roy, M.N., 99
Russell, Maud, 126
Russian Revolution, 59
Russo-Japanese War, 49

Schluter, Herman, 79
Schomburg, Arturo, 95
Scottsboro Boys, 75
Second International, 48
Silvina, Mary, 9
Smedley, Agnes, 69, 126, 129
Social Democratic Party (Germany),
    19, 48
Sojourners for Truth and Justice, 113
Souls of Black Folk, 12, 16, 23, 32–7,
    50
Southern Negro Youth Congress, 108

Soviet Russia Today, 108

Stalin, Joseph, 3; liquidation of Comintern, 94, 107; death of, 119–20, 121

Stalin-Hitler Pact, 108

Stalinism, 3, 6, 57, 87, 99, 101

State capitalism, 120

Stockholm Appeal, 111

Stoddard, Lothrop, 50

Streator, George, 77

Suez Canal, 129

Terrell, Mary, 25

Time Magazine, 123

Treaty of Versailles, 32

Trotsky, Leon, 67, 87, 119

Trotter, William, 24, 38, 42

Truman, Harry, 107

Tse-Tung, Mao, 3, 121, 129, 131, 134; support for Black liberation, 133, 138, 139

Tuskegee Institute, 23, 38

Universal Negro Improvement Association, 61

Universal Races Congress, 45, 49

Van Wienan, Mark, 71, 76

Vietnam War, 149

Wallace-Johnson, Isaac, 96

Walling, William, 42; *Russia's Message: The True World Import of the Revolution*, 58

Washington, Booker T. 23, 38, 39; *Up From Slavery*, 39

Weber, Max, 10

"We Charge Genocide" petition, 1; civil rights group, 2

Weinbaum, Alys, 71

Wells-Barnet, Ida B., 24, 25

Wilberforce University, 21

Wilkins, Roy, 145

Williams, Eric, 93

Williams, Robert, 133

Williams, Henry Sylvester, 25, 29

Wilson, Woodrow, 5, 45, 49, 148

World and Africa (Du Bois book), 86, 102, 124

World Partisans for Peace Conference, 110

World Peace Congress, 113, 114, 118

World Trade Union Conference, 94, 96

Wright, Richard, *Native Son*, 28; *Black Power*, 99, 130; *The Color Curtain*, 130

Yergan, Max, 109

Zhou Enlai, 131

Zimmerman, George, 2